BISON
BOOKS

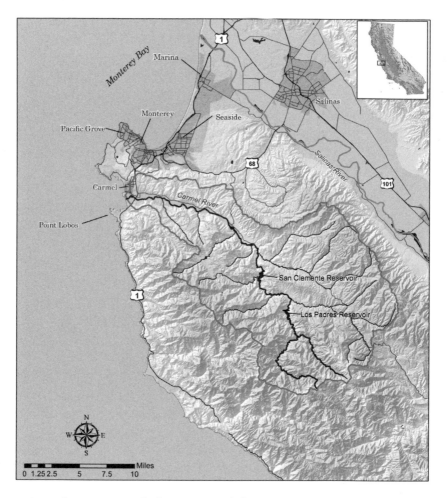

Carmel River watershed. Courtesy of the Monterey Peninsula Water Management District.

LEGEND

— Carmel River

☐ Carmel River watershed boundary

RIVER IN RUIN

THE STORY OF THE CARMEL RIVER

Ray A. March

UNIVERSITY OF NEBRASKA PRESS ⟩⟩⟩ LINCOLN AND LONDON

Library of Congress Cataloging-in-Publication Data
March, Ray A., 1934–
River in ruin: the story of the Carmel River /
   Ray A. March.
   p. cm.
Includes bibliographical references.
   ISBN 978-0-8032-3834-3 (cloth: alk. paper)
   1. Water resources development—California—
Carmel River Region—History. 2. Water-supply
—California—Carmel River Region—History.
   3. California, Northern—Environmental
conditions—History. I. Title.

TC425.C355M37 2012   333.91'620979476—dc23
2011028916

Set in Aldus by Bob Reitz. Designed by A. Shahan.

In memory of my mother,

ILONA MALOSH MARCH

who would drive the family car up
Carmel Valley on a warm spring day
and find a quiet place on the north bank of
the river and contemplate its passing waters

1603

A river of very good water but little depth, whose banks are well peopled with black poplars, very tall and smooth, and other trees of Castile and which descends from high white mountains.

SEBASTIAN VIZCAINO, Carmel River's discoverer

1945

The Carmel is a lovely little river. It isn't very long but in its course it has everything a river should have.

JOHN STEINBECK, *Cannery Row*

2009

Other than the Sacramento–San Joaquin River Delta, the Colorado River, and the Truckee-Tahoe water systems, the Carmel River water system is probably the most actively and complexly managed water system in California. This is a consequence of how little water there is to allocate, the attempts to avoid environmental harm, the endangered species present, and the multiple jurisdictions involved.

KEVAN URQUHART, Senior Fisheries Biologist, MPWMD

CONTENTS

ILLUSTRATIONS

PREFACE

The Carmel River presents a remarkable test case for a messed-up river. Almost everything that can go wrong with a river system through human activity has happened. What we see in the Carmel River is an archetypical manifestation of what happens in western rivers. | DR. ROBERT CURRY, geologist, 1981

In March 1999, the year I began my research for this book, the Carmel River made an ignominious debut before a national environmental audience when it appeared on "America's Top Ten Most Endangered Rivers" list. Declared endangered by the national advocacy group American Rivers, the relatively unknown Carmel River was now in the company of such notorious household names as the Klamath, Rio Grande, Mississippi, and Los Angeles Rivers.

How could this have happened to such a quiet, almost private, unassuming little river immortalized in prose and poetry by such famous writers as Robert Louis Stevenson, John Steinbeck, and Robinson Jeffers? Unfortunately, the Carmel River, like its giant cousins, is also under the pressures of supply and demand for its clear, clean, drinkable waters, while simultaneously being degraded and polluted. Though limited as a freshwater resource, the Carmel River is the primary supplier for residents, tourists, agriculture, and industry on California's rapidly growing Monterey Peninsula.

In listing the river as endangered, American Rivers, which is dedicated to the protection and restoration of North American streams, cited urban sprawl, water withdrawals, and dams as the principal reasons for the river's demise. Threats to the river's future health included "overpumping, nonpoint source pollution, continued development in the floodplain, the proposed development of a new dam on the river, and the need for greater public awareness of issues affecting the river."

How did the Carmel River get in such miserable shape, and what is being done to correct it?

To answer part of that question, the Monterey Peninsula Water Management District hired Dr. Robert Curry, a University of California–Santa Cruz environmental geologist, to gather information for a river development plan. When Curry arrived in 1981, the river stood beyond hope of restoration to the free-flowing stream of its past. For the water district, maintenance of the stream meant control of siltation and erosion due to fires in the watershed. In effect, because of the increase in sedimentation, the river was fatally eating away at its banks. Curry fingered numerous culprits responsible for the river's death stance.

Sedimentation was Curry's specialty and each culprit on his hit list related to all the others: fire suppression, dams on the river's mainstem, anadromous fisheries, human population and development along the river's unstable banks, the steep gradient of the river's watershed, groundwater extraction from the river's aquifers, and an active geologic-fault history that changed the river's course. He said that fire suppression, the actual extinction of the fires in Los Padres National Forest, where much of the Carmel River's watershed is located, only led eventually to larger fires. The result of larger fires meant more siltation deposits in the river. Sediment from fires ran off the watershed's steep mountainsides and filled the reservoirs behind San Clemente and Los Padres Dams, methodically reducing their storage capacity. He noted that a previous silt release from the reservoir behind Los Padres Dam resulted in a steelhead fish kill. (One solution for siltation buildup in the reservoirs is the use of prescribed, or controlled, burns.) Further culprits in the river's degradation included groundwater extraction from the river's aquifer and an active geologic fault that historically changed the river's course.

Three years into his study of the river, Curry issued a report concluding that an excess of sediment in the river caused riverbank erosion, a domino-effect condition that caused the river to widen its stream. The principal reason for the excess sediment was overdraft of the aquifers in the riverbed. Although not specific, Curry also blamed "human activity" for the river's incessant problems. Sounding an early alarm, Curry predicted that it would take twenty years to narrow the river channel, revegetate the riverbanks, and maintain a high water table. The California-American Water Company (Cal-Am), the major user of groundwater from the aquifers, disputed his assertions, countering that river vegetation died off not because of overdrafting but because of the 1976–77 drought.

Virtually all of Curry's culprits contributed to an undercurrent of inflexible debate between growth, no-growth, and controlled-growth factions. Proponents of prescribed burning in Los Padres National Forest ran into opposition from public agencies fearful of air pollution. Proponents of another dam on the river argued that water supply should not be used to control growth and were met with the opposing view that a new dam was clearly a pro-growth tactic. Owners of upscale homes along the river were reluctant to accept an additional water fee for restoring eroding banks and argued that they were being asked to pay more than their fair share. While Cal-Am debated the issue, extraction of groundwater from aquifers in the riverbed continued, vegetation continued to die, and the river's channel continued to change course. Politicians and public officials took opposing sides on whether another dam should be built on the river. Against a background of constant growth, the river became the victim of a social and political tug-of-war. The irony in the story of the Carmel River lies not just in the fact that so-called progress systematically destroyed the river, but that the river is an integral part of the Monterey Peninsula's social and political makeup, a famous central California locale that traditionally prides itself on environmental awareness and beauty for beauty's sake.

Curry was one of several notable scientists contracted by the Monterey Peninsula Water Management District (MPWMD) to research and analyze the river. He was to study sediment loading and erosion. Others were to study surface hydrology, groundwater, river vegetation, and fisheries. They included Dr. Luna Leopold, retired director of the U.S. Geological Survey; Dr. Tom Maddock Jr., retired chief theoretician of river systems for the U.S Geological Survey; and Dr. Herb Skibitzki, one of the leading groundwater experts in the United States. The intense interest from the scientific world provided a clear indication that the problems and challenges facing the Carmel River were the same for other rivers worldwide. An eventual, comprehensive management plan for the Carmel River could easily apply to river systems in other western American states and such places as the Soviet Union, India, South America, and New Zealand.

The Monterey Peninsula Water Management District paid $230,000 for a river management program in 1981, representing only a fraction of the various monies devoted to studying the Carmel River. Curry estimates that the Carmel River, as an intensely studied stream-flow system, received a considerable portion of the $2 billion spent on California river restoration since 1980. Like a patient with a fascinating exotic disease, scientists probed, examined, and administered the Carmel River from its origins to its lagoon with fishery plans, restoration plans, the replacement of spawning gravels, and stabs at watershed management. Volunteers on horseback and anglers packed baby steelhead to safe upstream drop points deep in Los Padres National Forest. Former artichoke fields became new estuaries, channel banks stabilized, and the breaching of the sandbar at the lagoon returned more closely to its natural form. Still, the river remains in intensive care.

Curry's assessment of the Carmel River's health is a dire

message, begging the question, Can the river be saved? The answer lies both in the story of its ill fate and in the growing awareness that there must be a balance in the demands we make on our natural resources, limited as they are. The story of the Carmel River is a lesson we must all learn if we are to save our rivers.

PROLOGUE

On a summer evening between semesters at college, my friends and I gathered at Undertow Beach near the lagoon where the Carmel River enters Carmel Bay. The evening was nippy, a high fog hovered overhead, so in a tight protected valley of sand carved out long ago by an old cable-driven dredge we built a little campfire of driftwood and drank rank red wine. Above and behind us loomed the shrouded gray wooden shed of the abandoned sand plant where, when it was in operation, the dredge returned its load of sand from just offshore to be dumped down a chute into a waiting truck below. The old squatter who used to live in a shack hidden by bushes next to the sand plant was gone. Perhaps evicted, even his shack was gone. So we were bothering no one, intruding only on the night, the waves crashing in front of us and the limits of our adventure. One of us thought we should see if we could get the dredge running. Like little boys angrily breaking sticks, there is a surfacing of bravado and desire for momentary violence that wine conjures in young men. Illuminated by a burning rag, the girls watched us start up the engine of the dredge. Then we randomly shifted long, iron levers back and forth and drove the dredge and its jerking cables out onto the sea floor and back again, snuffing out the fire in the little valley of sand like a puff of breath on a match. And then we were through. Spent. Disinterested. The campfire gone out and the valley of sand cleanly dredged, we left.

The next day, after sleeping in late, I learned that the old, dilapidated sand plant had burned down. It didn't take long for the sheriff to find a lost identification card belonging to one of us, and the whole story came out. Heroically shielding the girls who had been there, as was expected in those days, we took full blame and all financial responsibility. We would divide the damages between us; whatever they were. But not all of us had the money, and the choices we were offered were few. We could find ways to work and repay the rich owner of the old sand plant or we could join the army. Two of us joined up. Many years later at an official class reunion, I announced facetiously that our high school class, Carmel High of 1953, had been given an environmental beautification award for burning down the old sand plant. Everyone cheered and applauded. Now at that site at the mouth of the Carmel River, near its lagoon, there is a California state beach. It is called Carmel River State Beach. Where the sand plant once stood is a bank of public rest rooms. We still call it Undertow Beach, but we don't go there often.

In retrospect, life on the Carmel River was an idyllic time, a romantic time, as summers of our youth so often are when we reflect back on those unencumbered years. Idealistically, those of us who relied on the river trusted that it would be there forever. We were intimately familiar with the river, but sadly, with that intimacy eventually came a community neglect. At the time, it was something we failed to see, even in the irony of rewarding ourselves a fictitious environmental beautification award.

In its natural state and near its birthing grounds, the Carmel River is a playful thing. It begins rather unnoticed as a damp spot on a hot day before it travels any distance and picks up the meager contributions of two anonymous tributaries at its headwaters. The little tributaries surrender their scarce waters to the young river and they quickly lose all physical identity. This is the genesis of the Carmel River.

The first tributary flows from springs in the Ventana Wilderness at Divide Camp, just off the Pine Ridge Trail and west of the Church Creek Divide, which marks the ridge dividing the watershed of the Arroyo Seco to the south from the Carmel River watershed to the north. The second unnamed tributary begins as a vague seepage before pooling and is important to hikers and horseback riders because it runs year-round. It is a good, reliable watering hole before the now-formed Carmel River and its accompanying foot trail drop into Pine Valley. This miniature valley looks like a high Sierra Nevada landscape. A quiet meadow encloses the river flanked by tall ponderosas. In its spring bloom the valley's center is field upon field of lupine, poppy, larkspur, and mugwort along a little feeder creek that runs to the Carmel River. The meadow is so quiet that the levels of sound are distinguished only by distance: buzzing flies, several species of birds, and in the far distance the air itself almost creates the feathery breeze of a small, full creek winding its way through the tops of the trees. Descending from the wilderness, the Carmel River becomes an ethereal thread that verges on thought.

As the terrain continues to drop, the river cascades over an exposed rocky surface. There are two waterfalls less than a mile from Pine Valley, both known as Pine Falls. The upper downspill appears about one hundred yards before the Carmel River makes a southward turn. The second is just below a bend. The first drop is about fifty feet high and falls partly free. The lower is more a chute than a fall. In country that is unforgivably hot and dry in spring and summer, these falls carry the exotic aura of nearly attained tropics. There are river stretches here that teem with shadowy wild trout a foot in length. For twenty-one miles the river flows in relative privacy between inaccessibly steep canyon walls, making cameo appearances only in willow openings and at occasional pools. It keeps to itself until it runs quietly through the region known as Cachagua and a meadow once owned by a ranch cowboy by the name of Henry Barnes. There used to be an old cabin here.

Now, in place of the cowboy's cabin, stands the earth-filled Los Padres Dam, thirty feet wide across its top, seven hundred feet across at its base, and as tall as a thirteen-story building, built by California Water and Telephone Company in 1948. The dam and its reservoir fill the open space at the canyon where the Barnes Flat meadow resided, forming an enormous triangular block on the riverbed, anchored to the sides of the canyon's walls. It is easy to imagine the heft of excavation, the immense digging and lifting of soil to form the water blockade, but it's difficult to picture the lovely little valley and the meadow called Barnes Flat.

Just below the Los Padres Dam, where the river struggles to re-create itself on its journey to the ocean, there is a natural pool where on scorching summer days, kids swim or take turns on a rope swing. The pool is a cool and shady refuge because the sun can't penetrate the overhanging oak trees. On the bank overlooking the river, there is an old rock house that dates back to about 1920. Locals refer to this place simply as Rock House. Not too many people outside this region called Cachagua know of it.

Continuing below the dam, the river glides past Syndicate Camp, a private enclave formed in Charles Crocker's time of 1889. For the next six miles, the river starts to regain itself, flowing unobstructed in its wandering course to the ocean, until it reaches its intersection with San Clemente Creek. The early Spanish explorers named this little tributary for Saint Clement, the third pope and bishop of Rome, who discovered through a miracle a clear spring of water on a barren island. Perhaps the Spaniards also thought they were seeing a miracle when they witnessed this tiny tributary dribbling into a river not much bigger than the tributary itself. Whether Charles Crocker knew the Spanish tale remains unknown, but this is where he decided to construct the earliest dam on the river in August 1883. He used the same labor force to build this first dam on the Carmel River that he used to build the transcontinental railroad: Chinese immigrants.

The creek and the river, one not much bigger than the other, intersect in a steep, scrub-studded canyon that can be extremely hot and dry in August. Heat collects in the narrow drainage and only dissipates when the afternoon breeze travels up the valley and enters the canyon. There is a persistent dryness in the arid soil and the chaparral is covered with a thin layer of dust, regardless of how close the nearly turbid waters of the river and creek may be. Crocker's Chinese Dam changed the canyon and filled its mouth up, sometimes with opaque water, sometimes with more silt than water, and the heat and dryness remain.

To the uninformed eye, the Chinese Dam, as it became known, no longer exists. Its water-collecting reservoir is gone. The dam and reservoir were replaced thirty-eight years later by the larger San Clemente Dam, just six hundred yards upstream. In less than four decades, the combined tourist and population growth on the Monterey Peninsula pushed the demand for water beyond the capacity of the Chinese workers' efforts. Below San Clemente Creek and its namesake dam (constructed in 1920), the river makes another swing westward toward its eventual destination, washing and slowly crushing into a high embankment that carves out Camp Steffani, the first of three swimming holes in this section of the river and named after a Swiss immigrant who settled there in 1888.

The summer we graduated from high school, four or five of us decided to camp overnight on a narrow stretch of river beach at Camp Steffani. We swam in the afternoon, drank some beers, made a campfire, and lolled into evening. By the time the campfire was out, so were we, until there was a screeching scream upriver. Bolt upright, we all knew what it was, even though we yelled, "What was that?" It was a mountain lion, we were certain. Early the next morning we foolishly started upriver, keeping arm's distance apart so we wouldn't lose sight of each other in the willows. The cat's tracks were there on the wet bank, not a hundred yards from where we had camped. To bolster our false bravery we climbed up the steep, rocky cliff trail and went into the Bucket of Blood, a roadside bar on the old former stage trail that connected the village of Carmel on the coast with the small settlement of Jamesburg in the Santa Lucia Mountains. There, at The Bucket, we rolled dice with the bartender and with our winnings ate pickled hard-boiled eggs and drank illegal beers for breakfast. We told our story of the mountain lion encounter over and over to each other, and anyone who would listen, until it was perfect. A vineyard now occupies the site where the Bucket of Blood once stood above the Carmel River.

Where the river next makes a hard right turn downstream at the base of a bedrock bluff there is another large, deep pool. Or more correctly, there once was a deep plunge. It's still called Porter's Pool by the local kids. Porter's Pool is an old Carmel Valley Village name for a deep ponding in the river at the base of the cliff where the historic Porter home in Robles Del Rio stands. A small hand-built rock dam backed the river up to fill the pool and kids swam their horses in its deep waters. After the 1995 floods, the entrapment filled with sediment and turned the pool into a riffle. Maybe someday it will scour again.

Now the river passes under Rosie's Bridge that connects Robles del Rio, a 1926 subdivision, to nearby Carmel Valley Village. The bridge plays a significant role in the lives of those who live near it. It is the upstream boundary for steelhead fishing and where locals go to watch the river at flood stage. In the summer, boys and girls go there to catch crawdads or play children's make-believe games. One of those girls returned more than forty years later to scatter her mother's ashes under Rosie's Bridge. And it was another of the girls who played in the shallow summer waters under Rosie's Bridge who fell in love with the river. She frequently went to this particular spot to play out her dreams. She was a third grader when she knew she wanted to study riparian vegetation, though it was doubtful she understood the meaning of those words. One night at a slumber party, she and her girlfriends flicked the television channel back and forth to *The Invasion of the Body Snatchers*, but they were too scared to watch the movie at any length. During their channel hopping, they landed on Humphrey Bogart and Katherine Hepburn in *The African Queen*, where they safely settled in. The next day, the little girl and her friends climbed down the trail under Rosie's Bridge to play in the shallow water of the Carmel River. There they reenacted their version of Bogart and Hepburn slogging their way through the chest-high African waters, picking imaginary leeches off each other. From that moment, she was hooked. Today she is a plant biologist.

About fifteen miles from the sea, the now-adult Carmel River becomes fully engaged, though most often moving slowly, historically meandering seaward over Carmel Valley's flat lands with each flood. The river flows over an alluvial fill of sand, gravel, and some silt and clay lying between strata, and then it squeezes through a bedrock constriction, which the locals first called the Narrows. This tightening occurs at Scarlett Road, upstream of the golf courses at Carmel Valley Ranch and Robinson Canyon Bridge. The Narrows refers to the geographic feature where the walls or flanks of Carmel Valley narrow into a kind of bottleneck. The bedrock can be seen aboveground where the valley physically narrows. Below the surface of the river, there is a kind of parallel narrowing forming another bedrock bottleneck that actually separates the alluvial aquifer at this location on the river into upper and lower sections. The Narrows can actually "pond" water underground and slow the flow from the upper valley into the lower aquifer, a hydrological miracle of sorts. This is the reason a perennial streamflow can occur above the Narrows, when below or downstream the river can be bone dry.

A classmate of mine grew up with the river. Her grandmother's place in Mid-Valley was called Berwick Orchards, and her grandmother's property line ran to the middle of the river. The girl had a favorite spot in the riverside cottonwoods where her family went for barbecues and picnics. She believed that before the dams were built, this sandy section of her grandmother's place was part of the old riverbed. She patched up old inner tubes, floated downstream, and walked back over hot rocks, struggling to keep her balance. As the summer passed and the pools of water separated from the main stream, she looked for hatching tadpoles and watched them transform into baby frogs. When she was old enough for a horse, she rode a trail along the river and visited her friends up and down the stream. This was the shorter path, and it kept her away from the road. The river was her companion. It was pretty, peaceful, and quiet as it flowed along beside her. In the winter, that all changed, especially after a big rainstorm. Then the family would hop in the car and drive to where they could watch the swollen, muddy river rushing by. Her horse trails were now underwater, and sometimes the water even rose higher into the cottonwood trees. The river would try to wreck the Farm Center Bridge and flood her grandmother's lower fields.

Before the Monterey Peninsula's population sprouted, the valley floor and riverbanks supported a growth of willows, sycamores, cottonwoods, and other varieties of vegetation that in turn provided a safe and rich habitat for wildlife and steelhead, helping retard erosion of the riverbanks. Downstream and west of the Narrows, the river carries on, picking up sedimentation on its way, just like in the 1861–62 big flood, and shifting its wide but shallow channel by a half mile or so, if that is its inclination. In those days, it nonchalantly separated itself and then rethreaded as it flowed to the ocean. Today, as it enters its lower reaches, it glides smoothly over a huge aquifer where Robinson Canyon Creek joins up.

About a quarter of a mile before the Schulte Road Bridge, there is a bedrock outcrop and Steinbeck's Pool. The thirty-foot-high outcrop controls the meanderings of the river in this portion of its floodplain. The stream slams into the bedrock, forcing itself into a sharp ninety-degree turn, which causes it to scour out a deep rift in the coarse cobbles and gravels of its bed to form a pool. The gravel bar flanking the pool gently slopes down from the floodplain area. This became a 1980s riparian restoration "demonstration site" with the planting of a willow-and-cottonwood forest after excessive groundwater drawdown damaged the vegetation and severe floods uprooted them.

In John Steinbeck's novel *Cannery Row*, Mack and the boys came here to catch frogs for Doc's party. As Steinbeck described the scene, the boys drove a Model T truck, borrowed from Lee Chong, up Carmel Hill—backward. The carburetor gave out, and to keep gas feeding into it, they drove up the long grade in reverse. When they finally got to Carmel Valley Road, they turned inland and drove a few miles up the valley. According to Steinbeck's story, they went down to a spot where the river undercuts a high, overhanging cliff with a deep pool and sandy beach at its base. Mack and the boys waited there until dark to catch the frogs. Steinbeck's Pool sits strategically placed between two large production wells sunk by the California-American Water Company. Unless drought conditions cause the channel to go completely dry, fish and other stream-dependent creatures can find refuge here. Recharging the aquifer that supplies these wells with good, early winter flows, the river heads for its lagoon and a meeting with the ocean. Approaching its lagoon, the river has efficiently drained 225 square miles of watershed.

Water for the lagoon comes from whatever surface flow the river brings with it, but also from groundwater making its way into the river from the surrounding hills and little drainages. Reaching the lagoon, which is formed by a sandbar or dune berm between it and the ocean, the Carmel River comes to a rest. The berm forms above the ocean's high tidemark in late spring through the summer months when the wave action brings sand from offshore, causing a gradual buildup of a natural barrier between the fresh and salt waters. Unrestricted, the lagoon naturally extends back upstream, covering a broad area that includes pastures on the south bank and many of the houses built on the north bank. To enter the ocean, the river meanders slowly back and forth across the sandbar until it finds a giving outlet, but the landscape of the lagoon has changed from a meandering waterway and wetland habitat for birds and steelhead to backfills for a subdivision on the north side and new or expanded agricultural land on the south. The lagoon has become pinched in, constricted in its natural path to the ocean.

Today at the mouth of the Carmel River a giant underwater canyon, called the Carmel Submarine Canyon, connects to the Monterey Submarine Canyon on the other side of the Monterey Peninsula, indicating that the ocean may have once been three hundred feet lower. Today's modern river didn't carve out the canyon, but the proto–Carmel River, the prehistoric stream, must have been much bigger, or the landscape much steeper, to have excavated such a deep underwater canyon. And now there is a little bedrock sill across the river's mouth that must not have been there when the giant submarine canyon was carved out because the erosion would have cut through the bedrock that's just below the surface. There is a theory that because of faulting action, this area along the California coast is actually moving northward and that the bedrock sill has been shifted into place by plate movement, by tectonic activity, after the submarine canyon was excavated. It is this bedrock sill that saves the entire mouth of the Carmel Valley from saline water intrusion. It actually acts as a dam, blocking ocean water from moving inland and affecting the aquifer's water quality. But in eons past, the river's entry into the ocean must have been spectacular. The evolution or filling of this canyon sill may also explain why the beach, known among us old-timers as Undertow Beach, is so dangerously steep at the river's mouth. Monstrous, sneaky winter waves crashing on the steep embankment of the beach create a subsurface flow, or undertow, which can effortlessly drag unsuspecting strollers helplessly down the path of a former three-hundred-foot waterfall to an almost certain submarine death.

This is the story of the Carmel River as I know it.

RIVER IN RUIN

1 〰 SPANISH ERA

Vizcaino to Father Serra

It is mid-December 1602.

Idled in a thick coastal fog, the three Spanish ships wait for favorable weather to continue their journey northward. The ships and their crews have been at sea more than eight months with only an exploratory stop at San Diego. The men are sick with scurvy. Many have died. One ship is the *Santo Tomas*, a multideck commercial galleon of immense size. The second ship is the smaller frigate *Tres Reyes*, a square-rigged warship. The third is the *San Diego*, the fleet's flagship. Sebastian Vizcaino, a fifty-nine-year-old explorer and leader of the small fleet, is aboard the *San Diego*. He is searching for a port that can safely harbor Spain's Manila Fleet from pirates and storms on its way from the Philippines to Acapulco.

Windless in the fog, only the distant lolling sound of surf washing ashore reaches the ships and their crews. In the dense gray light, there is no hint of a shoreline that might hold a safe port for anchor. When the fog finally lifts, Vizcaino orders the ships to stand nearer to shore so he can see if there is a harbor. What he sees instead is a mountain range rising abruptly out of the ocean. The mountains are high with white ridges that turn reddish at the edges and are covered with woods. He calls the mountains Sierra de Santa Lucia and then sails north past the mouth of a little river emptying into a small bay. A Carmelite friar aboard the *San Diego* notes in his journal that the river "falls into the sea among rocks." The ships round the tip of a peninsula and at last drop anchor in a large harbor. The next morning, December 17, the fog is back and the weather is bitter cold, but Vizcaino, his expedition, and three Carmelite friars, go ashore and offer Mass under a gigantic oak tree. Not far from the oak is a fresh spring where they replenish their dwindling supply of water. Vizcaino rests his crew for nearly two weeks while he maps the immediate terrain, noting its animals, people, and the general lay of the region. He claims the land in the name of the king of Spain and he names the large bay where they are at anchor after his benefactor, the Count de Monte Rey, viceroy of New Spain.

On January 1, 1603, the temperature drops so low that the springs freeze. Two days later Vizcaino and a small contingent, including the three Carmelite friars, hike southward over the hill from Monterey Bay looking for freshwater. There, on the other side, they discover another, smaller bay where a "river of very good water but little depth" flows to the sea. Vizcaino asks the friars to give the river a name and they call it El Rio de Carmelo in honor of Our Lady of Mount Carmel, their patron and the expedition's protector.

Vizcaino's discovery of the Carmel River more than four hundred years ago set in motion the eventual development of California's Monterey Peninsula, which ultimately placed relentless demands on the region's only source of freshwater—the Carmel River. His discovery of Monterey Bay meant that Spain's galleons would have a safe port on their return voyages to Manila. Unfortunately for Vizcaino, advancements in the design and building of faster ships reduced the time it took to cross the Pacific and his discovery of Monterey Bay as a stopover port and source of freshwater from the Carmel River became unnecessary. As a result, his maps of El Rio de Carmelo and the region languished in the files of the colonial bureaucracy in Mexico City for 160 years before early colonization of Alta California began.

The Spanish did not return to Monterey and El Rio de Carmelo until 1770, when Gaspar Portola arrived overland from San Diego with orders to build a fort at a site overlooking Monterey Bay. A week later Father Junipero Serra, founder of the mission chain in Alta California, arrived by ship, anchoring in Monterey Bay and going ashore at the same spot where Vizcaino and his expedition landed 168 years earlier. Father Serra's instructions were to convert the Indians into loyal, obedient subjects of the Spanish crown, and on June 3, 1770, he established the Mission of San Carlos Borromeo de Monterey. However, it didn't take him long to realize that he needed freshwater to fulfill his assignment. The practical link between freshwater and converting Indians to Catholicism was agriculture. The Spaniards' method of converting Indians and colonizing the region was based on the growing of crops, enough to feed a presidio of soldiers and a future population of Indians. But Serra soon learned that freshwater for crops did not exist at the Monterey beach where the Spanish ships off-loaded supplies. The lagoons at Monterey yielded brackish water that the soldiers used for drinking but the lagoons were far below the elevated fields the Spaniards intended to irrigate. Freshwater from springs came from ravines higher up, but it was not sufficient to irrigate crops. Facing a water dilemma coupled with less than fertile land for growing, Father Serra decided to move his mission from Monterey and rebuild on the other side of the same hill Vizcaino and his expedition trekked nearly two centuries earlier, where more fertile land was plentiful and the freshwaters of El Rio de Carmelo flowed. However, before he could make his move Father Serra needed permission from the viceroy of New Spain. That permission arrived in May 1771, and in December Father Serra established a second mission on the Monterey Peninsula, this one on a barren hill overlooking El Rio de Carmelo. He named his new mission San Carlos Borromeo del Rio Carmelo, after the river, and for Saint Charles Borromeo. He planted corn, barley, and wheat.

This simple act of farming would eventually lead to Father Serra's becoming the first white man to turn to the Carmel Riv-

This watercolor by William Smyth depicts Carmel Mission circa 1826, five years after Mexico gained its independence from Spain. By 1834 the missions throughout California were secularized by the Mexican Congress and gradually fell into ruin. Courtesy of the Monterey Public Library, California History Room and Archives.

er for its water, a river that begins as seeps and springs in the steeply rugged Ventana Wilderness of the Santa Lucia Mountains. For its entire length, the river flows mostly shallow with little depth through banks of willows and crumbly sidewalls to a sandbar that blocks its entrance to the sea during the summer months because the river doesn't have enough strength to push its way through to the open ocean. When this happens, the river backs into itself and forms a lagoon. Father Serra planted his garden of corn, barley, and wheat upstream from the lagoon. To be successful he needed a three-mile irrigation canal to transport water from the river to the crops, but for reasons unknown, little progress was made in tapping the Carmel River, and for the next six years Father Serra relied on rain for irrigation. Finally, in desperation, he sent a plea on June 1, 1777, to the viceroy of New Spain in Mexico City, asking for meat and bread to feed the Indian workers. In his letter to the Viceroy he revealed:

While we have worked harder than ever to sow a large acreage, my judgment is that we will not have a third of the wheat that would ordinarily be expected. And so, in order not to be dependent, as we have been until now, on the rains, and the excellence of the land, which is indeed great, we have for more than a month and a half now, been busy with the help of more than thirty workmen leading off the water of the Carmel River more than a league away. As a result we will be able to irrigate as much ground as the mission will be capable of putting under seed for many years to come.

While hopeful, Father Serra pleaded for help, adding, "If we succeed in this enterprise, as I hope we will, not only will our troubles cease, but we will even be able to help many others in their difficulties. But this year we may have some difficulty in maintaining the Indians. Their hard work not being sufficient this time to maintain them, if I were allowed to get whatever bread and meat the frigate has no use for, and which on its return to San Blas would be wasted, I ask Your Excellency to consent that it should be given to us out of the love of God."

Another four years passed, and little progress was made in bringing water from the Carmel River to the mission fields. Father Serra was blamed for commonplace crop failures and widespread famine because of his inability to devise a workable system to draw irrigation water from the river. At one point even the plentiful steelhead in the river were not enough to feed the mission Indians and Father Serra sent them back into the Santa Lucia Mountains in search of food. He knew many of them would not return. It was unimaginable that irrigating with water from the river could be so difficult.

Nor was it predictable that men would argue over which method was best for transporting water from the river to the fields, but that's what happened in 1781. A mission padre and his native workers had nearly completed an irrigation ditch leading from the river to the fields when a more experienced farmer and former soldier, Don Ignacio Vallejo, was hired as steward to oversee the growing of crops at Carmel Mission. Instantly, a dispute arose between the two men when Vallejo stopped work on the padre's irrigation ditch. Vallejo put the Indians to work on a second ditch running parallel to the first. Although the first ditch was nearly complete and ready to bring water from the river to the padre's cornfields, the second ditch took seven months and the growing season was over before it was completed. The crop failed, but Vallejo's ditch was a belated symbolic success.

In spite of laboring to bring water from the river to the mission's fields, Father Serra's efforts to establish a mission on the Carmel River and another in Monterey never took a firm, lasting hold. The conscription of Indians and their conversion to Christianity was an important element in Father Serra's plan for the creation of an indigenous society dependent on agriculture. But so was their physical labor, and as their numbers decreased because of deaths from such diverse causes as poor nutrition, lack of access to medicines and over work, so did Father Serra's source of labor. By 1790 the Indian population at the two missions went into a gradual decline that would last for the next three decades, a decline directly proportionate to the Indian mortality rate, particularly among children and women of childbearing age. By 1800 Spain's interest in colonization was waning. In the meantime, attention to the Carmel River as a source for life-sustaining water went largely unnoticed and undeveloped.

Eighty years after Father Serra's frustrating efforts to grow crops at the Carmel Mission, the dispute over two irrigation canals carrying water from the Carmel River was irrelevant. Mexico gained its independence from Spain in 1821. The missions throughout California were secularized in 1834–35 and land held in trust for the Indians by the Spaniards was returned to them only to be lost to white swindlers seeking their fortunes during the gold rush of 1848. In 1849 California's constitution was drafted at Monterey's Colton Hall and for many years the prospering town was the only port of entry for taxable goods shipped into California by sea. A whaling station was established on the beach in 1855, where grays and humpbacks were butchered for commercial uses. In the 1850s and 1860s, Congress returned some of the original mission lands and buildings to the Catholic Church but by then all the missions were in ruin. By 1861 Carmel Mission, considered one of the most architecturally beautiful of all the missions in California, barely stood among its fallen ramparts. Cattle roamed freely past a broken stone baptismal font. Thousands of ground squirrels nested in adobe walls. An old garden reverted to a wild barley field and subsisted on its own. Only some pear trees lingered—as they do today—in a mission side yard. As Father Serra's Carmel Mission lay in decay, settlers with Anglo family names like Wilson, McDougal, and Finch were establishing ranches along the banks of the Carmel River, and drawing water from it grew barley in cultivated fields just upstream of the old mission. Wild oats covered the hillsides.

Father Serra and his procession of missions, including his efforts to irrigate with water from the Carmel River, was finally setting in motion the colonization of California and the establishment of a European civilization, tenuous as that civilization had been for more than a half-century. The Carmel River, discovered, then seen as an early resource before being abandoned and ignored, was still in Monterey's future.

2 〰 CROCKER ARRIVES

Tourist Trade Begins

"Right here. This is where we'll build the hotel," ordered Charles Crocker, as he jammed his walking cane into the soil that would become the foundation ground for the Hotel Del Monte and the future of the Monterey Peninsula. It was 1879. Crocker was immensely rich and powerful when he arrived in Monterey with his plans to turn it into a grand-scale tourist resort.

Crocker was one of the Big Four, the notorious railroad developers of the Gilded Age and builders of the western portion of the Transcontinental Railroad. Like his three partners—Collis Potter Huntington, Leland Stanford, and Mark Hopkins—Crocker, lured by the prospect of making his fortune, came west to California during the gold rush. Like the other three, he became a successful Sacramento merchant, and as he prospered, he helped found the California Republican party. It was through politics that he eventually met Hopkins and then Stanford and Huntington. Crocker was only thirty-nine years old when he and his partners took control of the Central Pacific Railroad and became its founders in 1861. Stanford was just thirty-seven and governor of California. Huntington was forty, and Hopkins the oldest at forty-eight. By the time Crocker, in particular, looked at the financial prospects of building the Hotel Del Monte and developing the Monterey Peninsula, he and his partners were multimillionaires, accustomed to unharnessed success and profits. It was Crocker who was largely responsible for pushing through the Transcontinental Railroad, and it was Crocker who was the force behind the modern-day concept that top-quality resort promotion with accompanying residential development would attract high-dollar buyers to the Monterey Peninsula. If successful, Crocker, now fifty-seven years old, would add social prestige to a list of entrepreneurial accomplishments that already included vast power and wealth.

When Crocker arrived in Monterey there were just two or three streets, covered with sand from the nearby beach; and in the rainy season they turned into rivers. There were sections of boardwalk elevated above the streets, but no streetlights. The houses were made from whitewashed or mud-colored, unbaked adobe bricks. There was no water system. Many of the buildings, including old army barracks, a government house, and military prison, were abandoned. Plaster fell off the walls of the formerly important Custom House. Bit by bit the town was falling into ruin. The most apparent signs of any social activities were at the saloons, or when the vaqueros rode the streets at a full gallop. Once a week there was a public ball, and frequently, fandango parties were held in private homes.

The town of Monterey was rich in natural beauty with its crescent-shaped bay and pine-covered hills. However, an economic and moral decay had set in since its glory days when, under the rule of Spain and then Mexico, Monterey flourished as the capital of both Alta and Baja California and then, in 1849, as the site of California's Constitutional Convention. The slow slide into decline began just as the town reached its peak. Its first setback was the gold rush of 1848, when men left Monterey in search of new riches. Then, at the Constitutional Convention held in Monterey in 1849, San Jose was chosen to be the first state capital—instead of its host town. Sacramento, with the gold rush literally in its front yard, became a commercial distribution point, taking more business away from Monterey. Sacramento didn't become the state capital until 1879, but by then it was well established and politically entrenched. San Francisco, also benefiting from the gold rush, became the state's major coastal port. Meanwhile, Salinas, twenty-five miles inland from Monterey and naturally suited to serving a growing agribusiness, became the county seat.

To European immigrants and first-generation Americans looking to strike it rich, Monterey had turned into a lazy Spanish town, bankrupt and drained of its population and commerce base and unable to support itself. Its population in 1880 was 1,662. In the view of the few hopeful merchants who had remained after the town's decline, the only inhabitants were Mexicans who spoke Spanish, lived the life of "mirth, music, and mañana," and harbored resentment against the invading gringo. Added to this perceived inertia was an assortment of residents who were against any further growth of the town. In effect, to the Yankee, there was no energy and ingenuity to return Monterey and its meager population to a sound capitalistic footing. The Mexicans dealt among themselves with iou's that might never be paid, and virtually all the land surrounding the town was owned by U.S. citizens.

Monterey was the perfect setting for Crocker's opportunistic hotel venture. Economically weakened and desperate for development, the town's business leaders were ready to make a gift of raw land to anyone who would build a first-class hotel on it. Their only condition was that the hotel's builder must invest his time as well as his money, and stay for a year or two. The burghers of Monterey admittedly saw their town as bankrupt and inhabited by non-English-speaking Mexicans, but they had other visions. Looking past an idle town of crumbling adobes, as Crocker did when he arrived, they saw a healthy climate, the possibility of mining, ranching, dairying, commercial fishing, and thousands of acres of undeveloped, undivided land. All they asked for was a hotel or two, perhaps a racetrack and a bathhouse on the beach in the sophisticated French style to attract visitors. But they also had a second motive in enticing Crocker to work with them. Crocker's arrival in Monterey was timely not only in the sense that he represented the future of the struggling town, but the local leaders also saw Crocker as a catalyst in their long-standing effort to get out from under the control of David Jacks, an intensely disliked land magnate. Before Crocker appeared with the promise of an extended railroad and luxury hotel, Jacks had amassed a land empire that included much of the town of Monterey, and at his peak, another ninety thousand acres in the county. He was politically connected in Sacramento, had served as Monterey's treasurer, and during his rise in power had orchestrated state legislation that stripped Monterey of its all-important standing as an incorporated city. This weakened the local government in its ability to provide services funded by property taxes. As late as 1891, Jacks continued to inflame public opinion against him when he refused to give an easement through property he owned so that a pipeline carrying water from the Carmel River could be extended to a land-locked parcel under someone else's ownership.

On the other hand, Jacks was an important benefactor of the Methodist Church and once, before Crocker's Pacific Improvement Company's entrance, donated acreage to the church for the establishment of a religious retreat. But with Crocker's willingness to buy considerable amounts of land, including property owned by Jacks, for real estate development, and the Southern Pacific Railroad's (also owned by Crocker and the Big Four) potential for bringing a line to Monterey, local business leaders saw an opportunity to dislodge the monopoly Jacks held on them. So when Crocker came to Monterey there was an immediate municipal sigh of relief, and as one newspaper commented, "We are glad to see that Monterey has at last got old Jacks' No. 11 boot off its neck, and is entering on an era of great business prosperity." What would follow Crocker's arrival, the business leaders foresaw, would be retail stores and subdivided land. And they had just the right piece of property for a first-class hotel. It was called Toomes Grove, and it consisted of 114 acres. There was ample room for a large, elegant hotel, a bathhouse at the beach, and eventually a racetrack. A. G. Toomes, who had arrived overland in Monterey in 1843, from New Mexico, agreed to deed the property to Richard P. Hammond of San Francisco, who was the agent for Crocker's Big Four. F. S. Douty, secretary of the Pacific Improvement Company, the landholding subsidiary of the Big Four's vast interests, requested the recording of the deed, and on January 17, 1880, the Pacific Improvement Company, with Crocker at the helm, took title to Toomes Grove. The purchase price was $5,301. Workers started construction on the hotel the next month.

At the same time that Crocker's agents were signing the papers to purchase the Toomes Grove property in Monterey, Crocker was thinking about how he was going to supply water to the new hotel. While he apparently believed that adequate water could be drawn from beneath the hotel grounds, the Carmel River was his obvious backup choice—but there was a costly problem in taking water from the river. Between the hotel and the river was the same hill that both Vizcaino and Father Serra had traversed before him. Because the fall of the river was so slight, at an estimated ten feet per mile, it was virtually impossible to pipe the water over the hill. A pipeline had to be tunneled through the hill at an estimated thirty thousand dollars. The cost was too high, even for Crocker, so trusting that water could be found on the hotel grounds, he gave up the idea of tunneling water from the river to the hotel and ordered that a well be drilled on site. Construction of the hotel and the drilling of a well began simultaneously.

Portly, but dressed in the formal corselet of the period—layers of dark suit, high-buttoned shirt and tie, and buttoned vest—Crocker spent much of his time at the construction site, as he had during the building of the Transcontinental Railroad, when he rode the line urging the Irish and his "Celestial" laborers, as he called his Chinese workers, to lay more track. Crocker saw himself as a hands-on investor whose personal presence motivated his workers. The hotel would make money and that prospect, in turn, motivated him. He was at the construction site daily, wandering through the public rooms and watching every nail being driven into a resort hotel that would be unmatched in the West in its size and grandeur. When he wasn't conducting personal inspections of the construction's progress, he parked his horse and carriage and watched from a distance. Just one hundred days after Crocker's groundbreaking declaration, the grand Hotel Del Monte cast an imposing shadow over the Mexican town and changed it forever. Waiting across the road from the hotel's entrance was the Southern Pacific's connecting rail line. Few voices, except for one, raised any objection to the change facing Monterey and its future. That came from an unknown writer at the time by the name of Robert Louis Stevenson, complaining in 1880, "Monterey is advertised in the newspapers, and posted in the waiting-rooms at railway stations, as a resort for wealth and fashion. Alas for the little town! It is not strong enough to resist the influence of the flaunting caravanserai, and the poor, quaint, penniless native gentlemen of Monterey must perish, like a lower race, before the millionaired vulgarians of the Big Bonanza."

Shortly before the hotel was to open, drillers found what appeared to be a good flow of subterranean water. Crocker's luck and timing were holding up, but not for long. The water quality was poor and a second well was ordered, but it too failed, this time because there was not enough volume. Drilling on the second well continued into 1882, and when it reached a depth of twelve hundred feet, the well was abandoned because there was no water to be found.

In the meantime, on June 3, 1880, Crocker's million-dollar Hotel Del Monte opened its ornate Victorian-Gothic doors to a rich and privileged class that would serve to make the Monterey Peninsula famous, and make Crocker even richer than he was. Prestige was his. After the hotel opened, it became Crocker's favorite ongoing project. A concentrated plan was set in motion to promote the hotel by bringing railroad officials, their families, and guests for frequent visits. They were followed by newspa-

Crocker's Hotel Del Monte, circa 1890, was virtually an overnight sensation. The hotel was built in one hundred days while crews simultaneously looked for additional sources of water. Courtesy of the Monterey Public Library, California History Room and Archives.

per correspondents friendly to the Big Four, who wrote regular society columns from the hotel's press room. Predictably, the positive publicity spread and wealthy patrons were soon booking the Southern Pacific's overnight Pullmans en route to the Hotel Del Monte. The resort was an instant success, and the social prestige that went with that success was Crocker's to hold. Now he turned to the logical matter of bringing reliable water to the hotel from the Carmel River.

Crocker learned the same lesson that Father Serra had more than one hundred years earlier, when he decided to move his mission from Monterey to a hillside overlooking the Carmel River: the ground beneath the Hotel Del Monte and the rest of Monterey contained little water of any quality. Monterey's local water supply was not going to support any form of civilization, either Father Serra's or Crocker's. After the opening of the hotel,

Crocker wasted no time in realizing that the logical place to look for water was the Carmel River. If the hotel was to be a catalyst for a fledging tourism industry, and the Monterey Peninsula to flourish with new homes and businesses, the water had to come from the river. A tunnel was too expensive, so there had to be another way to bring water from the river to the hotel—and to that end, Crocker needed the cooperation of Monterey's business leaders. That cooperation came on October 31, 1881, less than eighteen months after the hotel opened its doors to the public, when the town trustees unanimously adopted an ordinance granting the Pacific Improvement Company the right "to lay down and maintain a line of water pipes to convey water from Carmel River to the Hotel Del Monte." The ordinance was signed by S. B. Gordon, president, and H. Escolle, acting clerk. Escolle played still another role in Crocker's methodical strategy to systematically gain control of the Carmel River's waters when it came time to acquire actual water rights on the river. It was Crocker's Hotel Del Monte and its subsequent subdivision of lands, golf course expansion, and development of tourism that gambled on getting water from the Carmel River—and as time revealed, it wasn't that much of a gamble for years to come.

The significance of a pipeline agreement was twofold. First, by entering into the agreement with the Pacific Improvement Company, Monterey automatically defaulted any claim to a municipal water system it may have exercised at the time. The pipeline was a private venture funded by the Pacific Improvement Company—although some of its costs would be borne by users through rate charges imposed by Pacific Improvement's water company. Considering the nonexistence of a suitable water system and the willingness of the town's business leaders to reestablish Monterey as a growing city, it is understandable that they were receptive to a pipeline that initially didn't cost them a cent. Second, the act of granting a pipeline right-of-way to the Pacific Improvement Company indebted Monterey in such a way that the company became an instant benefactor, but not necessarily a benign one. The Pacific Improvement Company's landholdings in the vicinity of the town were enormous, and the company became an influential force in any direction Monterey chose to take as it expanded. This influence proved to be beneficial to the town, but there was always the lingering misgiving about whether what was good for the Pacific Improvement Company was good for Monterey.

Being a benefactor was nothing new to a company that used the straightforward description "improvement" (as in achievement or betterment) in the names of some of its subsidiaries. The Pacific Improvement Company was the Big Four's holding company for an incredible web of railroads and tracts of land, and Crocker and his partners were the controlling stockholders and directors. The company's earliest known records date back to 1869, a time when the U.S. Senate, with the House of Representatives not far behind, was well entrenched in an elaborate structure (some called it a scheme) of protective tariffs, national banks, railroad subsidies, appropriations, grants and bonds, and the giving away of millions of acres of land to railroad companies. In 1862 President Abraham Lincoln signed a bill incorporating the eastern arm of the Transcontinental Railroad, the Union Pacific Company, which would meet the Big Four's Central Pacific at Promontory Point, Utah, in 1869. Through the Central Pacific Railroad, the Big Four held over nine million acres of land given them by the federal government. In 1868 Crocker and his partners acquired the Southern Pacific and gained a monopoly over freight in and out of San Francisco and Oakland. By 1880, the year the Hotel Del Monte opened, the Southern Pacific owned one out of every ten acres of land in California. In this political milieu, the Pacific Improvement Company played a powerful role in the development of land through irrigation projects and railroad expansion in various parts of the United States, especially California and to a lesser extent in Texas and the South.

The Big Four had a strong, political and economic hold on

California and incalculable parts of the country as the free-wheeling entrepreneurial wave of the nineteenth century swept along, leaving behind a glorious Gilded Age in which U.S. corporations profited enormously from the often-illegal generosity of the states and Congress. With considerable business and political clout, what the Big Four pursued, it gained. If a town in California, for example, Visalia, refused to grant railroad privileges or objected to the Southern Pacific's strong-arm tactics, the railroad simply went around the town or built another town, such as Tulare.

The Pacific Improvement Company, the Southern Pacific's principal holding company, controlled the stock in various other railroads, including a Guatemalan railroad, and numerous nonrailroad subsidiaries such as the Monterey County Water Works, which would play a pivotal role in the development of the Monterey Peninsula and the extraction of water from the Carmel River. Other holdings included the Carbon Hill Coal Company of Washington State, the Ione Coal and Iron Company of California, the Geary Street Park and Ocean Railway Company, the Rocky Mountain Coal and Iron Company of Wyoming, the Oakland Water Front Company, the Southern Development Company, the Sonoma Valley Improvement Company, resort hotels in Monterey and Santa Barbara, and several steamships. Eventual ownership of almost all the land comprising the Monterey Peninsula, with the Hotel Del Monte as its magnetic attraction, was a minor, but favored, parcel in the Pacific Improvement Company's portfolio. Perhaps that is why few now remember that much of the Monterey Peninsula's development is virtually the legacy—the bloodline—of a consortium of four men led by Crocker, who were intensely disliked in California for their ruthless dealings and railroad monopolies. This was the company the business leaders of Monterey welcomed with open arms and subsequently were willing to provide with right-of-way easements through the town's public streets in order to bring water from the Carmel River to the Hotel Del Monte.

If there is irony in Crocker and the Big Four's reputation, it is in the fact that Crocker apparently applied none of the strong-arm techniques he was so infamous for in the railroad business to persuade Monterey's civic leaders to go along with his plans for their town. Granted, his wealth and reputation alone were enough to impress ambitious local leaders, but the relationship between Crocker and Monterey was, in effect, a comfortable marriage of mutual interests. The town's leaders wanted an investor who would not only give his money but also his time in support of their plans. Crocker was willing to do both.

In less than two years following the opening the of the Hotel Del Monte, it was apparent that Monterey did not have enough water of quality to sustain even the modest beginnings of a development plan, and Crocker's plans were far from modest. Crocker had right-of-way easements for a pipeline through the streets of Monterey, now all he needed was water in the pipe. It was imperative that the Pacific Improvement Company enter the business of acquiring water rights on the river and build a dam to store water. In doing so, the Carmel River became the fulcrum in a delicate balance between supply and demand.

3 〰 NOT ENOUGH WATER

Building the Chinese Dam

When Crocker first coveted its waters in 1880, the Carmel River was a simple, peaceful stream. It started high in the Santa Lucia Mountains as seepage that could be mistaken for leftover rainwater. It was so narrow it required no effort to step across it. As the river spilled out of the mountains and into its watershed, it gradually grew in size, but even then, it was a modest river. Only during the winters when heavy rains came did it become exceptional in its size and character, rushing over its banks and filling its floodplain. In times when few people were in its path, floods were not as threatening to property, and the river, free to roam, took its own course. Most of the time the Carmel River flowed continuously and peacefully to the ocean. And there were fish in the river. Steelhead trout returned from the ocean to their birthplace when the river would push away the ocean's sandbar and let the freshness of its waters mix with the salt of the sea.

Untapped and free flowing, the Carmel River was the obvious solution to the needs of Hotel Del Monte and the Pacific Improvement Company's plans for the development of the Monterey Peninsula, for the land adjacent to the hotel, and along the scenic coastline west of Monterey where Pacific Grove now sits. Accessible, and with no one claiming water rights to it, the river was the only rational answer. Crocker held an agreement with Monterey to run a pipeline to the hotel, but to deliver the water, a dam was needed to collect runoff from the Santa Lucia watershed feeding the river. Skirting both the hill between the river and Monterey and the original idea of a tunnel, a twenty-three-mile pipeline down Carmel Valley and around the tip of the Monterey Peninsula to the hotel would have to be trenched and installed. Two large reservoirs to store the water, first in Pacific Grove and later another one in Del Monte Forest, would have to be excavated and a pumping station or two built to move the water when gravity gave out. If this were an isolated local construction effort, it would have seemed formidable if not impossible to accomplish. But a pipeline and reservoir were minor engineering challenges for a railroad baron like Crocker who had already successfully driven men to move mountains in an incessant profit-minded fixation to build a railroad line through the Sierra Nevada. Although there was no competition to Crocker's dream of a world-class resort and the eventual development of the Monterey Peninsula, the strategy was to move swiftly in acquiring river access and the right to divert water from the Carmel River. In well-timed, tactical operations, the Pacific Improvement Company began to buy land in addition to what it already held in Carmel Valley, to acquire rights-of-way to the river, and to file water appropriation rights with the county recorder's office in nearby Salinas.

In 1881, the year the pipeline agreement was signed, the Pacific Improvement Company opened 17-Mile Drive at the tip of the Monterey Peninsula and began charging a twenty-five-cent-per-person toll; pedestrians were admitted free. Until then, and for some years after the opening of 17-Mile Drive, the undeveloped land was sparsely inhabited by Chinese abalone hunters and anglers. The area was conveniently secluded and gave a natural sense of privacy and limited access. It became known as Del Monte Forest, and its more popular and accepted image can be seen today in old photos of sheep grazing on what is now Pebble Beach Golf Links. A toll charge is still made of motorists who want to see the scenery and occasional mansions. Glamour was coming to the Monterey Peninsula, and Crocker and the Pacific Improvement Company turned the allure of paradise into real estate sales that continue the development of the Monterey Peninsula and its reliance on the Carmel River to this day.

In 1882 the Pacific Improvement Company bought the six-thousand-acre Rancho Los Laureles in Carmel Valley, a former Spanish land grant that was bordered on the south and the west by public lands and had extensive river frontage, water rights, and rights-of-way, including an eight-mile water ditch from the Carmel River to the ranch. Now owning more than thirty-eight thousand feet of river frontage, the Pacific Improvement Company made its initial stake on the river and gained access to a dam site at the junction of San Clemente Creek and the Carmel River. That same year four men, including Charles Crocker's eldest son, Charles Frederick Crocker, and a Southern Pacific engineer hiked the banks of the Carmel River looking for a site to build a dam. They chose the point where San Clemente Creek enters the river. On March 6, 1883, seventeen-year-old Lou Hare, along with three other Pacific Improvement Company employees, worked as a crewmember surveying in lower Carmel Valley. In his diary he notes traces of an "old Carmel Ditch—100 years old." He had discovered the remnants of the controversial irrigation ditch leading from the river to Father Serra's Carmel Mission.

To further insure its control over the river's water, the Pacific Improvement Company, on April 7, 1883, made its first water-rights acquisition. Filing for water appropriation rights with the County of Monterey, the Pacific Improvement Company claimed Carmel River water "to the extent of eight hundred inches measured under a four-inch pressure"—for conveying river water to Pacific Grove, Monterey, and the Hotel Del Monte. In acquiring rights to the river's water, the company was acting under an 1872–73 provision of the California Civil Code allowing that "the right to the use of running water flowing in a river or stream or down a canon [sic] or ravine may be acquired by appropriation." To establish a priority right to unappropriated water, the Pacific Improvement Company simply had to post a notice of appropriation at the proposed point of diversion, probably where San Clemente Creek joins the Carmel River, and record a copy of the notice with the county recorder. The only criterion for establishing and maintaining water rights on the river was that the water taken from it be applied to a "continuous beneficial use." The beneficial uses in this case were guests staying at the enterprising Hotel Del Monte, its lush gardens, its Laguna del Rey, and eventually its Roman Plunge. Under the appropriation doctrine, Title VIII, Water Rights, Sections 1410–1422, there is no requirement that water taken from the river be returned. However, the river water can be diverted "if others are not injured by such change . . . and may extend the ditch, flume, pipe, or aqueduct . . . to places beyond that where the first use was made." The diversion clause gave the Pacific Improvement Company the legal go-ahead to put water from the Carmel River into a pipeline that looped around the Monterey Peninsula and eventually ended at the Hotel Del Monte.

But filing for water appropriation rights and buying Rancho Los Laureles were not enough. There were numerous owners of Carmel River frontage with riparian rights, who had to be dealt with before the Pacific Improvement Company could safely and comfortably lay claim to the majority of the river water and its access. Riparian rights guaranteed landowners fronting the river their right to use the "full natural flow less upstream usage," but limited their usage to domestic and livestock needs. They could not use the water for irrigation. With the expertise gained in acquiring railroad rights-of-way across the West and in managing its irrigation projects in California's San Joaquin Valley, the Big Four's method of operation—in this instance with C. P. Huntington at the helm—was to act quickly and efficiently. Six weeks after the Pacific Improvement Company filed for water appropriation rights, on May 26, 1883, H. Escolle sold to Huntington "for $5 in hand" a pipeline right-of-way across his land to the river, in exchange for a water pipe and unlimited water.

The importance of this transfer of water rights is that H. Escolle was one of Monterey's business leaders who were anxious to see Crocker invest his money in the purchase of the Toomes Grove tract and build the Hotel Del Monte. He was a town trustee when Monterey signed over pipeline easements to Crocker. An immigrant from Salernes, France, Honoré Escolle was, at fifty-one, regarded as "the most energetic and rustling businessman in town and deserves a large share of the public business," according to a newspaper report. He owned a pottery business, a bakery, a general store, and thousands of acres not just in Carmel Valley but also in the Salinas Valley and in San Luis Obispo County to the south. He was a member of Monterey's township board of officers, and the town's treasurer. He had a significant investment in Monterey's commercial future and he was apparently willing to bank on that investment by selling water rights on the river to the Pacific Improvement Company. Selling his water rights to the company could easily be seen as not only a financial move on Escolle's part but a gesture of support for Crocker's ambitions to develop the Hotel Del Monte, and therefore Monterey, as a tourism center.

The Pacific Improvement Company now began buying up rights-of-way to the river and claiming water rights. Some riverfront owners sold for a dollar, others five to twenty-five dollars, depending on the length of their frontage. Most were willing to settle for small cash and use of the river water for their livestock and domestic needs. One landowner sold his water rights and right-of-way for the use of two water troughs and twenty-four dollars. Another sold for just a half-inch tap to supply both his livestock and house. No cash. The transactions do not reveal if the sellers thought they were being compensated for water they actually had use of under riparian rights. In 1883 and into 1884, the Pacific Improvement Company spent $811.36 on rights-of-way acquisitions. Ultimately, the company held majority control over access to the river and the water rights to divert water from the Carmel River around the Monterey

Peninsula and eventually to the Hotel Del Monte. Now the company was ready to build the first dam on the Carmel River.

It was Crocker, when he was general superintendent of the Central Pacific, who had insisted on Chinese workers to build the Big Four's Central Pacific Railroad. He started with two thousand Chinese laborers in 1865 and that work force grew to ten thousand in the last months of railroad construction. In the late 1880s, these Chinese immigrants—in spite of racial antagonism against them, harsh working conditions, and meager wages—were largely responsible for building most of the railroads in the West, including the Big Four's Central Pacific and Southern Pacific. Chinese workers had proven themselves on the Transcontinental Railroad. They were a flexible, mobile workforce, working separately and living separately from everyone else. When Crocker turned to the Carmel River as the principal water source for the Hotel Del Monte and the growing number of Monterey Peninsula consumers, he had nearly twenty years of experience working with his Chinese crews. Moving them about California as railroad work demanded, the Chinese were brought to work sites by the trainloads. In Crocker's mind, they were the perfect labor force to build a dam on the Carmel River—and the combination of water and Chinese labor was also perfect: one was essentially free and the other cheap. The Chinese workers arrived at the Carmel River in late August 1883, and the following month, where San Clemente Creek enters the Carmel River, and where the Spanish explorers had stopped to give honor to Saint Clement, they started blasting and cutting into the river's bedrock for the stone foundation of what would become the Chinese Dam.

Access roads to the river were built, and horses and mule teams hauled cement mix to the work site. It was predicted that the river's water would reach the Hotel Del Monte in early 1884. Simultaneously, work began on an eighteen-inch pipeline along the outer rim of the Monterey Peninsula, passing through what would become Carmel, Cypress Point, Pacific Grove, Monterey, and terminating at the Hotel Del Monte, giving rise to speculation that because valves were being placed at all the street crossings, the city would get any surplus water the hotel didn't use. In essence, Monterey, an unincorporated township with a board of officers representing the public's interest, was willing and eager to depend on a privately held water source. This reliance on private interests to supply water to the public spread throughout the Monterey Peninsula and exists to this day. Early dependence on the financially solid Pacific Improvement Company and its water company subsidiary would seep into the twentieth century. An outgrowth of this dependence, coupled with the enormous power the company and its successors wielded as major landowners and employers, created an amorphous company-town mentality on the Monterey Peninsula that while never clearly defined, never totally evaporated.

Still in the early stages of building the dam, the Pacific Improvement Company, fearful that seasonal rains might slow the work at the river, stepped up the construction schedule by putting crews on at night. The Chinese were working twenty-four hours a day. As construction of the dam continued on the Carmel River, forty to fifty workers were excavating for a new addition to the hotel. An eyewitness at the dam reported to the *Salinas Index* newspaper in October 1883:

> The dam is a strong and substantial structure built of marble and granite—both being close at hand—and cemented together with Portland cement. It is 6 feet wide at the top and 21 feet wide at the bottom. In the deepest part of the river there was 42 feet of gravel above the bedrock. The gate through which the water runs into the pipe is near the right bank of the river, and above it they are building a solid square tower of masonry in which is a floodgate to let off the surplus water. The tower will be 25 feet high, which will place its top above the river at its highest rise. The person in charge can go down the tower and see that the floodgates are all right. I

presume there will be a screen to keep the Carmel trout from going through the pipe to the reservoir back of Pacific Grove, or the anglers will growl, Salinas included. It is expected the dam will be completed the latter part of the week.

There was no fish ladder at the Chinese Dam.

On Sunday evening, October 14, 1883, at 6:35 p.m.—far ahead of the predicted schedule—the first water through the Pacific Improvement Company's pipes arrived in Monterey. The honor of getting the first pitcher full was accorded W. H. Pyburn, an Associated Press wire-service correspondent, and an unidentified *Monterey Argus* newspaper reporter. It took less than three months for the Chinese to build a dam on the Carmel River that historically would be called the Chinese Dam. It cost the Pacific Improvement Company $2,267.21. Water from the Carmel River was now running through a pipeline, making its bend near the tip of the Monterey Peninsula, before heading home through Monterey and to the Hotel Del Monte. The river, until now undisturbed and relatively undiscovered, except when it came to commercial uses, became a commodity of limitless "beneficial" use. A real estate boom was underway. Now the water had to be stored.

Plot-planned as a tiny Methodist retreat, Pacific Grove, on the tip of the Monterey Peninsula, was one of the beneficiaries of the publicity campaign fueling the Pacific Improvement Company's development strategy. Much of the land where the town sits was now owned by the company. With the completion of the Chinese Dam, domestic water was arriving at undeveloped residential lots, and sightseers on their way to 17-Mile Drive became convenient, ready-made targets for real-estate sales representatives. It wasn't long before the Methodist retreat was transformed into a hometown with year-round residents. The Pacific Improvement Company's scheme to buy unimproved land, bring water to it, and then sell real estate lots was taking hold. In 1884 there were one hundred full-time residents in Pacific Grove, but in the next two years the Pacific Improvement Company sold fifteen hundred summer-use lots, and the demand for water increased. In the meantime, the Southern Pacific passenger train, carrying tourists and hotel guests between San Francisco and Monterey, was shifting from a summer schedule to a winter schedule, departing Monterey twice a day for a five-hour, one-way trip. Tourism was not letting up just because the summer months had ended.

With the dam now finished and water from the Carmel River running through the pipeline, work continued on the Pacific Grove Reservoir. By November 1883 there were two hundred men and thirty-two teams of horses employed, in addition to other horses that were kept walking up and down the clay bottom of the reservoir to puddle it and pack it down tight so it would hold the water. Work on the reservoir was completed by the end of the year. Also in December, workers were busy laying three miles of pipe all through the Hotel Del Monte grounds for irrigation use. And, to give wastewater from the hotel an outlet to the bay, a sewer line was constructed connecting the Laguna del Rey, east of the hotel, with another lagoon closer to Monterey.

Four years later, in 1887, the Hotel Del Monte was destroyed by a fire that some say was started by disgruntled Chinese employees, but Crocker wasted no time in rebuilding. He reconstructed the second Hotel Del Monte exactly as the first, in all its Victorian splendor, except that two more wings were added. Hotel clientele increased, and so did the population of the Monterey Peninsula. In order not to lose any tourist business during the rebuilding of the Hotel Del Monte, another hotel, El Carmelo, in Pacific Grove, was built by the Pacific Improvement Company. When the Hotel Del Monte reopened, the 114-room El Carmelo became a second-tier hotel for the middle class at two dollars a day. Water was flowing from the Carmel River to the future cities of the Monterey Peninsula and, most importantly, to the Hotel Del Monte, but as development increased on the Monterey Peninsula so did the need for more water from the river.

By 1888, less than a decade into an ambitious design for developing the Monterey Peninsula, Crocker saw still another entrepreneurial dream come true. The Hotel Del Monte was well established, water ran from the Carmel River through his pipeline, the towns of Monterey and Pacific Grove were taking hold. On a personal level, the leaders of Monterey had adopted him and he had reciprocated. This man, whose wealth and social connections went from San Francisco to New York, now called Monterey his home. In every regard, the rebuilt Hotel Del Monte became Crocker's home away from home, and one he preferred because of its commercial and social contributions to his wealth and reputation. In fact, Monterey was his final home. Rebuilding the Hotel Del Monte, adding a second hotel in Pacific Grove, and overseeing plans for still another reservoir to store water from the Carmel River were the last efforts of a man who had achieved much in his life.

While Crocker was at the height of his career, he ignored his own health. He neglected his doctors' advice to slow down and diet. He was a sixty-four-year-old man who, at 225 pounds, was overweight and overworked, both self-imposed physical burdens. Two years earlier, in 1886, Crocker was seriously injured in a horse-and-buggy accident in New York. Uncharacteristic as it may seem, he was injured while drag racing.

The *New York Times* gave this account of the bizarre incident:

He went for a drive in a light road wagon to which was harnessed a pair of fast trotters fresh from the West. On the avenue he met Mr. D. O. Mills, who was also driving a spanking team of trotters. The two millionaires had a friendly brush up the road, and Mr. Crocker's team proved the faster. It was on the return that the accident occurred. Mr. Crocker was driving at a very fast gait and Mr. Mills was a short distance behind. Crossing One Hundred and Twenty-fifth Street the wheels of Mr. Crocker's wagon struck the double track of the cross-town railroad. The wagon bounded and the horses plunged with fright. Mr. Crocker was unseated and thrown out of the wagon. He fell partly on his right shoulder and side, and the back of his head struck heavily on the macadamized road. He involuntarily released his hold on the lines and was not dragged, but as he lay on the roadway insensible he was struck in the side by the wheels of his wagon.

Crocker was taken to Manhattan Hospital where he was diagnosed as having a concussion of the brain. One or two ribs had been broken, there was a severe cut on the back of his head, and contusions on his back and side. He recovered, it was reported, "in due season," but close friends thought the injuries only added to his subsequent physical disabilities. Publicly, Crocker scoffed at suggestions by journalists that he had not fully recovered from his injuries when he returned to the West Coast.

He retreated to the Hotel Del Monte in early August of 1888, certain that all he needed was a brief rest in the luxurious privacy of his creation. He had lived the good life of the Gilded Age—rich foods and a demanding, self-imposed regimen to make money before he made time for himself. To compensate, he belatedly began dieting. Then, knowing he was ill, he inexplicably decided not to use Dr. John P. Heintz, the hotel's in-house physician, nor did he summon his personal doctors from San Francisco. Instead he resorted to calling in Dr. J. I. Stephen, a member of the Royal College of Physicians of Ireland who had an office next to the post office on Monterey's lower-end, but commercially active, Alvarado Street. In a five-day period, from August 7 to August 12, Dr. Stephen wrote four prescriptions for Crocker.

Dr. Stephen's first prescription was for twenty-five grams of antipyrine, also called phenazone. Dr. Stephen recommended taking it with chloroform water. Antipyrine could be used in the way in which Tylenol (acetaminophen) is used today, to reduce fever, pain, shakes, and chills. Antipyrine is a weak, local anesthetic, but the practice of using it on the mucosa of the mouth, nose, and throat is now obsolete. Later that same day, Dr. Stephen followed up with a second prescription. It was a rhubarb tincture containing sodium potassium tartrate. The rhubarb was used as a flavoring agent. Apparently, Dr. Stephen suspected Crocker was ailing from gastrointestinal symptoms, most likely constipation. Three days later, on August 10, Dr. Stephen prescribed a codeine formula of twelve pills, each containing ten milligrams, an average dosage even by today's more conservative standards. The formula is usually prescribed to alleviate pain, coughing, or gastrointestinal discomfort such as cramping or diarrhea. On August 12, 1888, Dr. Stephen wrote his final prescription. The prescription called for ammonium carbonate, taken orally, one tablespoon every hour. Ammonium carbonate is the basis of smelling salts when inhaled. When taken orally, it probably was used as an expectorant. Crocker would be dead in two days.

It is possible, based on the contents of the four prescriptions, that Dr. Stephen thought he was treating Crocker for a cold and constipation when actually Crocker may have had fluid in his lungs, intestinal problems, or even congestive heart failure, a complication of diabetes. It is also possible that an ulcer could have been burning a hole in his stomach. Ultimately, Dr. Stephen's prescriptions were of little use. Crocker fell into what was reported at the time as a diabetic coma, and not even his Southern Pacific Railroad could carry his oldest son, Charles F. Crocker, and doctors to his bedside in time. On August 14, 1888, at 3:25 p.m. in the afternoon, and just a month before his sixty-fifth birthday, Crocker died alone at the Hotel Del Monte. The Big Four was now reduced to two surviving directors, C. P. Huntington and Leland Stanford. Charles F. Crocker, who was placed in charge of his father's $25-million estate, represented the Crocker family interests in the Southern Pacific. In 1890, two years after his father's death, Charles F. Crocker was elected first vice president of the South Pacific Railroad. While it's not clear when he took over as president of the Pacific Improvement Company, it is known that he resigned that position in 1893.

4 §§§ WATER DEMAND INCREASES

A Second Dam Is Built

As Crocker lay dying in his room at the Hotel Del Monte, construction of a second, larger reservoir was underway in the confines of Del Monte Forest. In August 1888, about one hundred Chinese workers were again called on to perform the labor of excavation, burning brush, cutting down pine trees, hauling them off, dynamiting the stumps that remained, and driving a ten-horse plow. By October their numbers had increased to a staggering seventeen hundred when the midday train carrying another three hundred Chinese workers arrived in Monterey. The main work camp was pitched at the north end of the reservoir under some trees. The Chinese encampment was a short distance away. However, within a week some of the workers were taken to Templeton, California, to extend Southern Pacific's railroad line further south. Templeton, south of the Monterey Peninsula and in San Luis Obispo County, was a two-year-old town and was named for Crocker's grandson. Originally, the town was to be named "Crocker." At the time the Chinese workers were sent there, Templeton was the last stop on the southbound Southern Pacific's railroad line. And, to the north across Monterey Bay, in Santa Cruz, observers were shocked at the Pacific Improvement Company's investment: Not only was the water supply system to the Hotel Del Monte and burgeoning Pacific Grove and Monterey already larger in size than Santa Cruz's, the company had also built a reservoir that cost more than the entirely new water system being proposed for Santa Cruz.

Everything was now in place: the Chinese Dam, the pipeline, the reservoirs. In a year the Southern Pacific increased its passenger schedule to three departures a day from Monterey, Sundays excepted. In 1889 Chinese laborers built a Southern Pacific branchline from Monterey to Pacific Grove, and with that the Pacific Improvement Company's holdings on the Monterey Peninsula were fully opened to development. Crocker's plan was irreversibly set in motion; the Monterey Peninsula was being transformed from a forgotten bypass to a major tourist destination that demanded more and more water from the Carmel River. Pacific Grove, becoming a religiously regulated town, was four years into a real estate boom. Monterey was expanding into neighboring New Monterey on one side and Oak Grove on the other, and there was pressure on the city to improve Alvarado Street, the main street. The Hotel Del Monte was booked to its Victorian rafters with the carriage trade.

What Crocker had started was now in perpetual motion: the original building of the Hotel Del Monte and its rebuilding (a reincarnation that took just six months), transporting tourists to the Monterey Peninsula by the Southern Pacific trainload, constructing the first dam on the Carmel River, trenching a twenty-three-mile pipeline and excavating a sixteen-million-gallon reservoir to capture the water, and most importantly, creating a publicity campaign that would become dogma for ensuing decades. But the publicity campaign would not have succeeded as easily without the local newspaper's zealous support for Crocker and the Pacific Improvement Company's plans. The fact that the weekly *Monterey Argus*, Monterey's sole newspaper between September 1883 and October 1888, when Crocker was putting his vast plan into action, was supportive of developing the Monterey Peninsula is one of the critical reasons—in addition to the support of the business community—why he was so successful. California newspapers at the time were rabidly partisan. Publishers had three political or editorial options. They were either Democrat, Republican, or Independent. The newspapers, unlike their modern successors, made no effort at presenting "balanced" news to their readers. An Independent newspaper, for example, did not necessarily adhere to party line, nor was it neutral. It would switch from one political side to the other depending on the publisher's view of what was best for developing the area. The *Monterey Argus* was Republican. The *Salinas Index*, twenty-five miles inland and the only competition to the *Argus*, was also Republican. If there was opposition to Crocker's development dreams, it wasn't obvious in the Monterey or Salinas newspapers.

An example of journalistic bias was the effusive reasoning disguised as reporting by the *Monterey Cypress* in 1888, after the *Argus* folded. The *Cypress*, another Republican newspaper, boasted in a headline (all in capital letters) "A GREAT RESERVOIR"—with a stack of subheads extolling the virtues of Crocker and his water "enterprise" and proclaiming "Monterey Rejoices." Underneath the headlines, the article included the support for not just a second reservoir of similar size to the first, but one that would serve a city of forty thousand people.

The water is now pouring into the vast hole at the rate of one thousand gallons per minute. When full, Monterey will have, with the old reservoir, 156,000,000 gallons of the purest water on the coast ready always in case of emergency. The water as it comes from the mountains first enters then into the smaller one, from whence it is served to Monterey, Pacific Grove, Del Monte, and the numerous small towns, which like magic have grown up in our vicinity. Truly, Monterey is blessed and the Pacific Improvement Company has proved a friend indeed. The work was conceived and put underway by the late Chas. Crocker and is one of the schemes of that great enterprising man and noble friend of Monterey.

The second reservoir, completed on December 7, 1888, was built at a cost of $175,000. It was 285 feet above sea level, covered 33

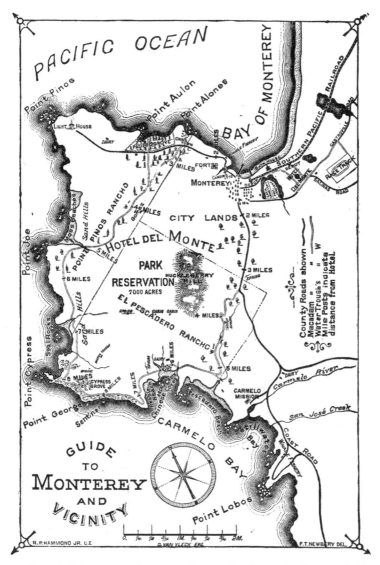

By the end of the nineteenth century, the Hotel Del Monte and its vast holdings, depicted in this 1899 promotional map by D. Van Vleck, was the center of the Monterey Peninsula's universe. The townships of Monterey and Pacific Grove were proverbial dots on the map and Carmel was still a dream. Courtesy of the Monterey Public Library, California History Room and Archives.

acres, was 217 feet deep, and held 140 million gallons of Carmel River water.

By 1918, a passage of just thirty-five years since the construction of the Chinese Dam, the tourist and population growth on the Monterey Peninsula had pushed the need for water beyond the capacity of the river's first barrier. That year, architect John Wilcox began drawing up plans for the Pacific Improvement Company to build another, larger dam on the Carmel River. By 1920 the population of Monterey was 5,479. That number nearly doubled by 1930. The capacity of the Chinese Dam and its reservoir system of 1883–84 was no longer large enough to keep up with the demand for water from the Carmel River. A second, larger dam was needed to replace the Chinese Dam in order to capture even more runoff from the Santa Lucia watershed draining into the Carmel River.

California, like the rest of the nation, was between world wars and in transition. The Progressive Era that gave politics back to the people in a belief that government participation was in their best interests, combined with a faith that humans had the ability to improve their environment, was ending. In its place, a Chamber of Commerce conviction that "corporate enterprise" was the best leader for economic development was sweeping the state from San Francisco to Los Angeles. An example was the formation of the California Development Association in 1921, which advocated cooperation between business and government, but only on the condition that government take a backseat. The California Development Association worked closely with state agencies responsible for water development, arguing that "poor" water development blocked economic progress. This was the mood of the state in 1921, and the Monterey Peninsula, on the cusp of a population boom, could hardly have missed it.

Just months before construction started in 1919 on a second dam—the San Clemente—California was in the last year of a three-year drought and Northern California was getting the worst of it. The statewide water inventory was the lowest on record, and even if the rains returned to normal so late in the season, a water shortage was predicted for domestic, industrial, irrigation, and power purposes. The drought was so serious that in late February 1920, the California Railroad Commission called a meeting of federal and state officials and representatives of virtually every power company in the state to discuss the problem of water supply and the possible need to curtail power deliveries. The threat of a curtailment imposed by the Railroad Commission was enough to prompt government officials to issue a joint appeal to every water user in the state in an effort to make the public-at-large aware of the importance of conserving water. "Individuals, as such, cannot cope with this situation," they said. "All must cooperate." And they asked that "water users lay aside their individual interests and join in a 'save the water' movement." Echoing the severity of the drought was the Coast Valleys Gas and Electric Company, which received power deliveries from Pacific Gas and Electric and in turn supplied power to the Monterey Peninsula. "This is a matter which is of grave concern to the residents of Monterey County," a power company official warned.

Rainfall statistics show the Railroad Commission was correct in its concerns, especially about rainfall on the Monterey Peninsula. In March 1920, only 8.84 inches of rain fell on the Monterey Peninsula, compared to 18.52 inches the year before at the same time. By mid-April, the total rainfall locally increased to 12.83 inches, but was down from 20.04 inches a year earlier. The typical rainy season for the Carmel River watershed and its dependent towns is between November and April, with 60 percent normally falling between December and February. By mid-April 1920, any hope of significant rain was remote. At the same time, the drought was becoming a serious threat to the residential and tourism growth of Monterey and its neighbors.

It was against this background that the building of the San Clemente Dam, which took two years to complete, 1919–1921, went largely unnoticed. A new dam to catch more water from the Carmel River was desperately needed, not only in response to the drought but to sustain the growth that had been set in motion by the end of the nineteenth century and the beginning of the twentieth century. The long-awaited time of prosperity was coming and it captured all the community's attention. A social conscience that might have objected to a dam was virtually nonexistent.

One reason for public apathy, or disinterest, over the construction of a dam on the Carmel River was that until the early 1900s, water users in California took what they wanted and, in taking the water, also took control of it. At times they filed notice of their appropriation with the county recorder, but no formal permission was required from any administrative or judicial body. In 1902 the passage of the federal Newlands Reclamation Act made water development even more attractive. The Newlands Act provided that revenue from the sale of public lands could be used for irrigation projects in both arid and semiarid regions. This led to the damming of nearly every major river in the West. Today it is administered by the Bureau of Reclamation. In addition to supporting irrigation projects, the Newlands Act inadvertently allowed the construction of river-based power plants supplying energy to most of the West's major population centers. It wasn't until 1913, and the passage of California's Water Commission Act, that today's permit process was established, eventually evolving into the California State Water Resources Board, with authority to govern California's surface water by a permit and license process. Real estate developers of the early twentieth century were still enjoying a carryover from the nineteenth century: The federal government, with states and local governments following, encouraged free enterprise with virtually no limitations. The legal system fostered private property rights and the environment was to be exploited as a commodity. In other words, "water that went unused was water wasted."

In contrast, under today's current law, California is authorized by the California Water Code to make inspections at its own expense of all dams completed before August 14, 1929. The code also requires that owners of dams built prior to August 14, 1929, file application for approval of such dams. But in 1918–21, when the San Clemente Dam was being designed and built, there were no permits as we know them today to be issued, no environmental impact statements or reports to be prepared or answered, no hearings to debate the dam's merits, and no political vote to persuade one way or another. Construction of the San Clemente Dam simply went forward, with scarce attention drawn to it except for rare announcements from S. F. B. Morse's Monterey County Water Works office. Morse had taken over the Pacific Improvement Company and its water subsidiary as a liquidation project in 1915, but in 1919, a year after Wilcox began drawing plans for the dam, Morse converted the Pacific Improvement Company into his own, privately held Del Monte Properties Company. The San Clemente Dam was a matter-of-fact water storage project that would provide more water for a water-hungry, demanding, and growing Monterey Peninsula. As a major construction activity on the Carmel River, it was a quiet effort that was ignored by the public and local press.

Even without the environmental watchdogs common today, architecturally, San Clemente dam is an imposing, if not unattractive, edifice. Its concrete structure curves inward and arches back into the reservoir behind it, creating an art deco illusion superimposed on an ancient and rugged tapestry of steep scrub oak and chaparral-covered canyons feeding dryly down to the river. Its backdrop of collected water skews the scene, however. The reservoir trap competes with the loose, nutrient-poor soil, and the grubbing roots of trees for the scarce moisture, sponging up whatever wetness it can collect in the unpredictable rainy seasons. The Carmel River and San Clemente Creek run nearly parallel before they merge behind the dam. Only a narrow spit of land, a small peninsula that rises above the water level, sep-

When the San Clemente Dam replaced the original Chinese Dam on the Carmel River, in 1921, it set in motion the altering of the river's flow by trapping sediment and causing incision on the mainstem, which led to unstable banks downstream. Today it is a destructionist symbol that environmentalists cite in their efforts to have it removed. Photo by Julian P. Graham, circa 1924. Courtesy of the Monterey Public Library, California History Room and Archives.

arates them. By 1960 the mouth or entrance to San Clemente Creek had almost completely silted up and reduced the reservoir's storage capacity because of erosion runoff from previous fires in Los Padres National Forest.

And what became of Crocker's dream for a luxury hotel, although dependent on water from the Carmel River, which would bring high society to the Monterey Peninsula?

In the decades of the 1930s to '40s, the Monterey Peninsula was between dams, but water projects were underway throughout the state as part of President Franklin D. Roosevelt's New Deal efforts to put the unemployed back to work. To the north was Shasta Dam, in Sacramento were two elevated water towers each holding three million gallons, south of San Francisco was the Pulgas Water Temple, and in Yosemite National Park the O'Shaughnessy Dam was enlarged to store more water in the Hetch Hetchy Reservoir for a growing San Francisco. And in San Diego, the original Civic Center was built on nineteen acres of tidelands and showcased a twelve-foot-high granite sculpture. The San Diego project was known as the Guardian of Water. Often these and other water projects in California in the late 1930s and early 1940s were architecturally stunning, in addition to being well engineered. The Pulgas Water Temple, for example, consisted of a number of fluted columns arranged in a circle and inscribed with the Biblical "I give waters in the wilderness and rivers in the desert, to give drink to my people." And in San Diego, the twelve-foot-high granite sculpture is of a woman holding an olla, or earthenware pot, symbol of the need to conserve water in Southern California.

The private sector was not to be outdone by the New Deal artisans and laborers. William Randolph Hearst had San Simeon Castle built between 1922 and 1939 just south, across the Monterey County line, in San Luis Obispo County. Fitting with the times, he, too, honored water as a symbol. The castle's Neptune Pool is engineered to withstand an earthquake by actually swaying with the seismic movement. Water flows to the pool from natural springs south of the headwaters of the Carmel River. It is also piped to two reserve tanks, one of 345,000 gallons, the other holding 1.2 million gallons. Below the pool is a large room housing an intricate sand-based filter system. The water is kept at a steady seventy degrees.

In 1915, well ahead of Hearst's Neptune Pool and the influences of the New Deal in California, the Roman Plunge at the Hotel Del Monte was added as a recreational attraction to the hotel's gardens and grounds. Its arrival symbolized something new. As the New Deal wound down, the Hotel Del Monte, burned in 1924 and rebuilt the same year as a Mediterranean edifice, was undergoing its own form of transformation and its own unique glorification of water: capitalizing on the celebrity of its guests against the exotic backdrop of the Roman Plunge.

By the early 1940s, the hotel was still as popular with the wealthy and their celebrity playmates as it had been from its beginning. The only exception was during the years of the Great Depression when room occupancy was understandably low. In the '40s, guests were uniformly making the most out of their recovery from financial hard times. They smiled and posed before the society cameras. The smart set applauded the aerial ballet divers at the Roman Plunge or watched the polo matches as if nothing ever changed, as if the glory days in paradise lived forever. In 1941, on the eve of World War II, the Roman Plunge at the Hotel Del Monte was an elongated, exaggerated swimming pool filled with salt water and frequently lined with spectators attending showy aquatic events. The Plunge was protected from the outside world by groves of trees, shrubs, and rich, expansive gardens. It was so large that when the light was just right, the pool reflected the entire east tower of the hotel, which was the bulk of the structure's Mediterranean form. It was large enough to reflect the stark white columns of the hotel's solarium, giving a Greco-Roman feel in its monumental scale and expansive scene, and therefore its name. All around the pool's edges were nautical ropes looped from white post to white post. In its flat stillness, the Roman Plunge was the forerunner of an infinity pool, timelessly classic. Every Sunday and Thursday at noon, couples dined Plunge-side at al fresco luncheons and on the lawn bordering the adjacent formal gardens with the impeccably groomed hedge maze. Men wore sports jackets or blue blazers, ties, and pleated slacks, and women flaunted summery print dresses reaching to just below the knee. They sat on wooden folding chairs on the sloping lawn that faced the solarium and its columns on the other side of the Plunge. They were there to be seen. The Roman Plunge and lavishly landscaped grounds of the Hotel Del Monte—irrigated with water from the Carmel River—had the aura of the rich, the privileged, the fashionable men and women of the late 1930s and wartime 1940s.

Prior to World War II, the Roman Plunge was the center for gatherings of high society at the Hotel Del Monte. When the hotel was sold to the U.S. Navy, the Plunge became a survival training pool for pre-flight-school cadets. Photo by Julian P. Graham, circa 1930. Courtesy of the Monterey Public Library, California History Room and Archives.

Innocent of an impending world war, a long parade of public worshipers came to see trendy health-conscious people take its waters, to feed the swans floating on Laguna del Rey, the hotel's artificially created lagoon, and to watch the diving exhibitions at the hotel's Plunge. The aquatic events were surreal moments in time as women in fashionable one-piece bathing suits and skullcaps, to protect their hair from the salt water, grasped Indian bows and arrows and sailed off the high diving platform. The divers were human still lifes, fixed in midair against the pure clear sky above the grand old hotel. It was a mock-archery ballet that never seemed to finish, and water was its symbolic stage.

At the northeast end of the Plunge there was a "sandbox," big enough but still intimate for a dozen or so sun worshipers to spread out their towels. With a glassed-in, French-paned windbreak along the windward side, anyone not a hotel guest was kept out while movie stars and the fashionably privileged men and women sunbathed protectively but not hidden from view inside the sandbox. The glass-paned windbreak was like looking at the celebrities through a transparent silver screen, but it also gave them an illusion of warmth as they sunbathed on white sand imported from the beach across the Southern Pacific railroad tracks from the hotel. They posed for publicity photographs that were sent to all the wire services, glamour magazines, and newspaper society pages with the enviable message that the Hotel Del Monte was the only place in the entire world to be. In 1942, a few months before the United States Navy took over the hotel before eventually buying it, movie star Lana Turner sat for photographs in the sandbox. She was innocently seductive in a black, one-piece, halter-top bathing suit, her blond hair pulled back under a print scarf, her nails manicured, a wedding band on her left hand and a Philco portable radio next to her thin ankle adorned with a gold bracelet. In the one quick but eternal moment captured by the photographer, Lana Turner symbolized what the Hotel Del Monte had so successfully accomplished in the years since Crocker opened its doors in 1880 and began the tedious challenge of taking water from the Carmel River. It was a secular Mecca in the grandest and most traditional sense. For more than sixty years, a relatively short period, the Hotel Del Monte's in-house promoters created an image built on foreign and Hollywood royalty and the wealthy, but not-so-famous society members who could afford the tariff—all supported by necessary water from the Carmel River.

With a ready acceptance that comes with new money (in Crocker's day it was new money, but by the 1930s that money was becoming established wealth, and by California's fast-track standards, it soon became old money), the hotel's guests over the years saw presidents William McKinley and Theodore Roosevelt come and go. Guests watched the aquatic exhibitions, horse racing, and dancing by Ronald and Roberta. They played polo, or clad in long camel-hair coats and fur-collared wraps, they watched the polo matches. They played golf with Basil Rathbone and Nigel Bruce, they played tennis with Charlie Chaplin, or they watched exhibitions by tennis stars Elizabeth Ryan and Big Bill Tilden. And they picnicked along the undeveloped 17-Mile Drive in the Del Monte Forest. Later they partied with Salvador Dali, rubbed shoulders with the Vanderbilts and poet Robinson Jeffers and his wife, Una, and they laughed at Bob Hope's jokes. These events, like the aquatic ballet, polo, and tennis exhibitions, were the Hotel Del Monte's interpretation of high-society gatherings, and they were used to advertise and promote the hotel. It was a passage of time unmatched and unequaled on the Monterey Peninsula in its excessive grandeur, and there remains a near-mythic legend that this surreal tableaux could only have happened on the Monterey Peninsula and at Crocker's Hotel Del Monte—courtesy of water from the Carmel River.

The Monterey Peninsula, and its imposing Mediterranean-style Hotel Del Monte of the late 1930s and early 1940s, was a setting that fed the public's imagination while the wealthy patrons of the hotel influenced another standard, one based on both real and perceived wealth. The Monterey Peninsula became a fantasyland. On a daily subconscious level that could surface at any time, reality was indistinguishable from the make-believe. Yet this was a manufactured world fueled by publicity. If everyone looked rich, then they must have been rich. And it made local residents feel rich, too. If they were told by the society pages that last weekend they witnessed the special people at play, the local residents felt special. If outsiders raved over the coastline or the quaint architecture, everyone looked at it afresh and raved, too. When they were told they were lucky to live in such a beautiful setting, they felt privileged and self-righteous. They listened to the worshipers and read the press clips and believed them. There was no doubt in their minds that they were inhabitants of not just an average imaginary fantasyland but of an incomparable natural setting, a paradise where the sun always smiled, where the canopy of trees was a heavenward altar, and where there was an endless supply of fresh mountain water from the Carmel River that they blissfully took for granted.

But as in a paradise misused, there was also a hidden, false air. The Hotel Del Monte appeared to be a resort-oriented venture with the ultimate purpose of serving its guests in the highest possible manner. But behind the facade of promoting the hotel on a national scale was a desire by the hotel's developers—first the Pacific Improvement Company and later the Morse-run Del Monte Properties Company and its Pebble Beach successors—to sell residential and commercial lots in Monterey, Pacific Grove, and the Del Monte Forest. Most of the Monterey Peninsula was prime real estate for the entrepreneurial Crocker and his successors. The exception was Carmel-by-the-Sea, which would undergo its own unique brand of development and needs for Carmel River water. Lana Turner, her predecessors, and successors, were merely used by the hotel and its development company as publicity vehicles to attract tourists to travel to Monterey on the Southern Pacific and entice potential real estate buyers to invest in paradise, all supported by water pumped through a pipe from the Carmel River. In its final glory days, life at the Hotel Del Monte was a contrived fantasy time, but everyone believed in it because so much propaganda had been set in motion by the time Lana Turner smiled in front of the camera. But behind the dramatic scene of a grand hotel and its alluring clientele was a critical dependence on freshwater and Crocker's original ingenuity to move it from the Carmel River to the Hotel Del Monte.

The glory days at the Hotel Del Monte did die. Lana Turner was one of the last celebrities to pose for publicity shots in the hotel's sandbox. A second world war began and the hotel's new occupants, the U.S. Navy, used the Roman Plunge and its salt water for training pre-flight-school cadets in war survival by climbing rope ladders that simulated the sides of battleships. When the war ended, the Blue Book social life on the Monterey

Peninsula shifted to the insulated protection of the gated Del Monte Forest and The Lodge at Pebble Beach, heir apparent to the Hotel Del Monte. By the mid-1960s the once reliable and revered Del Monte Express, Southern Pacific's passenger train, became part of Crocker's historic legacy. Even as Southern Pacific streamlined its equipment and changed its schedules, passenger rail traffic steadily declined. In 1963 the train service, which had brought so many tourists and hotel guests to the Monterey Peninsula since 1880, was looking for a polite way out.

"There isn't anything more that we can do," said R. M. Gilmore, general passenger traffic manager for Southern Pacific, symbolically throwing up his hands in despair. "The Del Monte has been a great part of the Monterey Peninsula. But it's a part of the past, and not the present—just as was the old Del Monte Hotel and other famous old landmarks. The train had a lot to do with helping people discover the Peninsula—perhaps it did it too well for its own good—as increasingly heavy auto traffic on the improved Monterey Peninsula freeways testifies so very well."

The Hotel Del Monte became history, Crocker's railroad passenger service no longer needed. The Chinese Dam became obsolete because it wasn't big enough to store the amount of water the Monterey Peninsula consumed. Population growth and its attendant needs for Carmel River water continued to climb as the popularity of the Monterey Peninsula became more widespread. True to Crocker's plan, water from the Carmel River flowed through the pipes that enclosed the Monterey Peninsula, and the need for freshwater increased incrementally. Dependence on the Carmel River was addictive. Somewhere in the midst of change—a change completely reliant on freshwater to sustain itself—the Roman Plunge, symbolic of the excesses of wealth, was emptied of its salt water and refilled with water from the Carmel River. The river was no longer innocent, no longer making a random run to the sea. But the story of the Carmel River takes an unexpected twist, and it could only happen in Carmel-by-the-Sea.

5)}} A VILLAGE OF ARTISTS

At Odds with the Pacific Improvement Company

As Monterey, with its Hotel Del Monte, was progressively moving toward establishing itself as a vacation playground with appealing real estate for purchase, Carmel-by-the-Sea was going through its own version of development. The two towns, separated by the hill traversed earlier by Vizcaino and Father Serra, were entirely different from each other in their social, cultural, and economic makeup, but they shared a common dependence on water from the Carmel River.

Frank Devendorf was president of the Carmel Development Company and cofounded Carmel with San Francisco attorney Frank Powers. When the two began their business relationship, Powers was the financial facilitator and Devendorf the manager. Eventually they worked out a partnership where Devendorf became a stockholder in the Carmel Development Company, and between the two of them, they held virtually all the controlling stock. Powers managed the business dealings out of his San Francisco office, trusting Devendorf to sell building sites and handle local matters in Carmel as the man on the streets of the newly formed village. From its beginnings in 1902, Devendorf and Powers had carefully groomed Carmel to fit their image of an intellectually based community nestled in an idyllic forest. They saw that trees were planted and that roads didn't interfere with the trees. They laid out an irregular town grid to avoid monotony. They purposefully recruited a particular type of "character" to live in their new town. There was a mutual

48

respect between the two men and a desire that the character of Carmel remain that of a small village of writers and artists, college professors and independent thinkers—people Devendorf called "brain workers." If the new residents of Carmel had a problem, they brought it to Devendorf for resolution. He was a seemingly benevolent man who loved both people and trees. As a developer he was an enigma. One of his closest friends was Perry Newberry, a controlled-growth advocate ahead of his time and editor of the feisty *Carmel Pine Cone*, a weekly newspaper. Newberry was also the village's recently elected mayor and, along with Powers and Devendorf, was soon to be a player in Carmel's theater of water.

Another player in the unfolding water drama was the Monterey County Water Works. Despite its public, bureaucratic-sounding name, it was the privately owned water company that supplied water to virtually all of the Monterey Peninsula. Its lineage went back to the legacy of Charles Crocker, when Monterey County Water Works was formed in 1905 by the Pacific Improvement Company and then reorganized in 1907. The Pacific Improvement Company deeded to Monterey County Water Works all the land at the original Chinese Dam, all the pipelines, except at the Hotel Del Monte, all the rights-of-way, easements, and right to divert water from the Carmel River, the Clay Pit Reservoir in Del Monte Forest, the Pacific Grove Reservoir, and a pump house. This arrangement lasted until 1916, when Monterey County Water Works deeded back to the Pacific Improvement Company essentially the same ownership arrangement, with the exception that the amount of water to be taken from the Carmel River in any one year could not exceed 35 percent of the total flow of the river. In effect, the Pacific Improvement Company and Monterey County Water Works were dividing the system and the burden of serving the water, according to a decision by the California Railroad Commission, which stated in part: "The amount of water which the improvement company under the deed may divert for its own uses is found . . . to be about the same amount which the company has . . . been applying to a beneficial use at its hotel, grounds, and ranches. . . . It proposes to . . . deliver into the 22-inch main of the water works . . . 65 percent of the quantity of water reaching that point, which will furnish sufficient water for the water works for several years to come."

This set the stage for the Pacific Improvement Company to eventually liquidate and sell off all its Monterey Peninsula holdings, including Monterey County Water Works, to S. F. B. Morse, a trusted and up-and-coming entrepreneur from the East, and in 1919 the founder of Del Monte Properties Company—spin-off successor to the Pacific Improvement Company. Morse became yet another power broker in the water dynamics of Carmel and the Monterey Peninsula. Like a dramatic plot in a play at Carmel's outdoor Forest Theater, the protagonists and antagonists were about to clash. And the central conflict, naturally, was water.

But first, some historical perspective is necessary to set the stage. Morse entered the Monterey Peninsula arena in 1915 as manager of the Pacific Improvement Company's "Del Monte Unit," as the Hotel Del Monte and Pacific Improvement Company's vast land holdings were called. He had just completed an eight-year apprenticeship managing the Crocker-Huffman Company, one of the largest privately owned irrigation systems in California, supplying water to farmers in the San Joaquin Valley, near Merced. Morse had also been closely involved in the formation of the publicly owned, not-for-profit Merced Irrigation District that drew its water from the Merced River flowing through Yosemite National Park. Before that, he briefly worked for fellow Yale graduate John Hayes Hammond, an electrical engineer who owned the Mount Whitney Power Company in Visalia, California. In 1904–5 Hammond's Mount Whitney Power built a number of dams to supply electricity for irrigation-using ground wells.

Morse was well matched for the Crocker empire; he knew

Templeton Crocker, who was a year behind him at Yale. Templeton Crocker was readily acknowledged as the richest student at Yale. Morse was class of '07 and distinguished as captain of Yale's national collegiate championship football team. He was a distant relative of the Morse code inventor. Templeton's lineage and connections could not have favored Morse more. Templeton's father was Frederick Crocker, an official of the Southern Pacific Railroad. His grandfather was Charles Crocker and his uncle was William H. Crocker, Charles's youngest son. It was Templeton who suggested that Morse get in touch with his uncle William; there might be a job for him out West. While not related by blood, S. F. B. Morse, eastern bred like all the Big Four, was a direct descendent of the Crockers' "old school." He loyally followed the Crocker interests in irrigation. By the time he arrived on the Monterey Peninsula, he was well versed in water rights and the internal workings of the Crocker power structure. As founder of Del Monte Properties Company, the successor to the Pacific Improvement Company, Morse was also president of its subsidiary, the Monterey County Water Works. Yale pedigree and first-hand field experience in place, Morse knew the importance of controlling water at its source, and the Carmel River was under his control.

The village of Carmel needed water from the river to support development, much like Monterey, with its earlier dependence on the Carmel River. Ironically, the river at this point actually governed or controlled the rate of growth on the Monterey Peninsula, because until the first dam was built and pipelines laid, there was little infrastructure in place to move the water from the river to where it was needed. It is also significant that pipelines carrying water from the Carmel River through Carmel and leading to the reservoir in Del Monte Forest and on to the Hotel Del Monte belonged to the Pacific Improvement Company.

Unless it found another way to get water from the river, the Carmel Development Company was faced with buying the water from the Monterey County Water Works. It's not surprising, given the frustrating history of drawing from the river, that water was Devendorf's bane, starting when he and Powers formed the Carmel Development Company, on November 25, 1902. Three days after incorporating, and responsible to a board of directors, their first item of business was to attend to the fledging town's water system. Powers had previously purchased nearly a thousand lots within what would become Carmel-by-the-Sea, plus another six hundred lots on eighty acres adjoining Carmel, and an eighty-nine-acre tract between the future village and the Pacific Ocean. He also owned almost a mile of white sand beach that had belonged to the San Francisco Glass Works, another 172 lots north of town, and a beach house that included a 145-foot-deep well with a pump at 80 feet supplying fifty thousand gallons a day. Powers sold his holdings at cost to the Carmel Development Company when it incorporated, making himself the majority stockholder. The Carmel Development Company had land but no water. The only alternatives, if Carmel was to take root as a developing village, were to find access to the Carmel River or drill a well. Powers and Devendorf decided to do both.

On March 6, 1903, the Carmel Development Company Board of Directors authorized Powers to contract with the Pacific Improvement Company for water. That was the first option. The second option was a river well. A year later, and under "threat of a water famine" that went unexplained, Powers and Devendorf reported back to their board of directors that they "had arranged with the Catholic priest, representing the archbishop, to allow us to sink a well in the fourteen acres owned by them near Carmel River." The church agreed that the Carmel Development Company could use the water taken from a site near Father Serra's Carmel Mission for twenty-five years. But there was a catch. The church did not want to sell any of its land. So Powers bought a neighboring one-acre lot for drilling the well. The new well, tested for two days at a depth of two hundred feet, brought in another fifty thousand gallons a day from the Carmel River aquifer.

The Carmel Development Company, despite its origins as a land development enterprise, was literally backing into the water business—just as Father Serra and his mission and Charles Crocker and his Pacific Improvement Company had. Neither Monterey, Pacific Grove, nor Carmel had sufficient groundwater to support their growing populations. Water had to be imported from the Carmel River or nearby wells in order to sustain development. The river well cost the Carmel Development Company five thousand dollars, and Powers recommended that the company should also own its water plant, which he was willing to finance and then turn over to the board of directors. Powers was directed to do whatever he deemed advisable, including the acquisition of land and water rights and the maintenance of a water plant, pumping, and distribution system.

Within two years the Carmel Development Company had installed two water tanks, one holding one hundred thousand gallons and the other twenty thousand gallons. It had rights-of-way, a pumping plant, and a distribution system through its own pipeline. Powers and Devendorf had also started a publicity campaign for Carmel with the appointment of a subcommittee to work on an advertising program to promote the new town not only as a summer retreat but also as a winter resort. They set a budget of one thousand dollars, with half going to billboard and streetcar ads and the other half targeting Southern California and using the Southern Pacific Railroad, with stops both in Monterey and Pacific Grove, as their vehicle.

"They are ready to assist us in advertising as much as they were Pacific Grove," Powers reported to his board, referring to the late Crocker's Southern Pacific Railroad system.

By 1904 the Carmel Development Company was considering trading the Pacific Improvement Company five hundred acres it owned within adjacent Pebble Beach for twenty thousand dollars in advertising support during one of the Pacific Improvement Company's eastern promotional tours, although it's not clear that the trade was ever made. A few months later, Powers did make a deal with Southern Pacific for its local railroad agents to distribute booklets and "cards," or flyers, extolling the virtues and property prices of Carmel. The booklets and cards, at ten booklets a town, were posted in 121 towns along Southern Pacific's California route. The development of Carmel was not going to happen by chance, any more than the progressive development of the Hotel Del Monte, Pacific Grove, and Monterey by the Pacific Improvement Company twenty years earlier had happened by chance. Tourists and potential property buyers would travel by the Southern Pacific Railroad to see Carmel just as they had when the Hotel Del Monte was being used to attract people. In less than a year, Carmel had a hotel, a store, livery stable, and its own water works—all managed by the Carmel Development Company. What Carmel did not have was the cooperation needed from its first option, the purchase of Carmel River water from the Pacific Improvement Company.

While the Pacific Improvement Company was willing to assist Carmel's cofounders in some matters, such as advertising support, it was not an entirely agreeable party to sharing or supplying water to the Carmel Development Company. Water negotiations with the Pacific Improvement Company hit a snag. In August 1905, Powers reported to his board of directors that the Pacific Improvement Company was moving to control rights-of-way for a water line across land owned by the Carmel Development Company and to begin taking water from wells in Carmel Valley. The board immediately authorized Powers to do anything necessary to protect its water rights. Powers went to work and at his year-end report to the board stated:

> We were compelled to inaugurate an injunction suit against the Pacific Improvement Company on September 3 to prevent them running a pipeline across our property and they have now offered us a very favorable proposition for compromise which is under consideration. As soon as we have compromised with Pacific Improvement and are satisfied that

the water works need not be further extended, we ought to be in a position to reduce our loan at the bank (Wells Fargo) and in a very short time be paying dividends.

The compromise Powers alluded to was apparently an agreement with the Pacific Improvement Company in which the Carmel Development Company would own certain water appropriation rights on the Carmel River but would contract with the Pacific Improvement Company for the actual supply of two hundred thousand gallons per day for "use in the territory including Carmel-by-the-Sea and vicinity." The water would be piped by the Pacific Improvement Company to a one-hundred-thousand-gallon tank on an eighty-acre parcel owned by the Carmel Development Company. "A water works and pumping plant has been installed and it is running very successfully," Powers told his board. "The water is of the same character as that usual for deep underground water, in that it is necessary to store it for forty-eight hours before it is freed from ferrous salts. We have been using it for over six weeks and there are no complaints of any consequence."

In its first five years of existence, the Carmel Development Company had carefully looked after its water interests. The company acquired various properties to ensure access to well sites on the Carmel River. It formed its own water company, installed pipes, a pumping station, and holding tanks. It even began looking at land south of Carmel that would later become Carmel Highlands and the potential water sources to supply an eventual development there. In that regard, one water source was San Jose Creek, draining into the Pacific Ocean south of Carmel, where the company bought three hundred acres that included over two miles of creek frontage. Most importantly, it had secured an agreement with the Pacific Improvement Company—option number one—to provide water from its pipeline to newly arriving Carmel residents. Powers and Devendorf had wisely decided in 1902 that they would explore both of the two obvious routes open to them in obtaining water for their new village—going to the Pacific Improvement Company and its existing pipeline system and to the aquifers of the Carmel River. At no time did it appear that they were overextending themselves in a profit-minded desire to expand Carmel. They were taking water where they could get it—from wells and from the Carmel River—but it had not been easy.

In 1913 Powers and Devendorf made a decision to get out of the water company business, and for $12,500 they sold the water plant to their old adversary, the Pacific Improvement Company. The sales agreement included all water rights held by the Carmel Development Company in Carmel Valley and its rights to water in the Carmel River. The Carmel Development Company could not sell any water from the river or its watershed for irrigation or domestic use. Among the sales terms were two contrasting items: One, an implied condition imposed on the Carmel Development Company that "no further differences, or embarrassments, should exist between the Pacific Improvement Company and Carmel Development Company." The reference was to the Pacific Improvement Company's requesting permission from Devendorf to run a Pebble Beach transit bus across what the Pacific Improvement Company's manager in San Francisco, A. D. Shepard, called a "dead line" at the Pebble Beach–Carmel tollgate. Shepard wanted to extend the bus route to Ocean Avenue, Carmel's main street, a few blocks downhill from the Pine Inn. Devendorf granted the request with the reservation that he could cancel it at any time. Shepard, sitting in his office in the Crocker Building, was miffed and complained to Powers. Powers sided with Devendorf, and in writing a letter to his man in Carmel, said: "You will note that Mr. Shepard no longer claims any specific agreement other than the proposition that we want to be entirely friendly. This certainly is what I want. Friendliness, of course, does not consist of giving them the right to use our property, whether a two-foot strip or any other matter provided it will entail a loss to us. That matter, of course, is under your department and whatever you do in that matter will be entirely satisfactorily to me."

Powers's use of "a two-foot strip" was a reference to Shepard's attempt to move a fence two feet in exchange for a strip of land that was in Powers's personal trust, called The Dunes, which was not under ownership of the Carmel Development Company. Powers had repeatedly explained to Shepard that the land in question was his personally and that he did not want to enter into an agreement with the Pacific Improvement Company that could be a conflict of interest, or would leverage the Carmel Development Company into doing something it did not want to do.

"He is certainly a fine crawfisher," Powers wrote Devendorf.

The second condition of the 1913 sale was that the Pacific Improvement Company would furnish domestic and household water to Carmel, including the Fourth Addition, and provide the water "with as good service and as reasonable rates" that it supplied the inhabitants of Pacific Grove and Monterey. Devendorf knew that clause intimately. On the wall of his office was a map of Carmel showing the Fourth Addition. It was outlined in red ink.

6))) CARMEL'S THEATER OF WATER

Enter Two Therapists from Oakland

On Monday, August 8, 1921, Anne Nash and Dorothy Bassett, with all their belongings in tow, boarded a southbound train for Monterey. The two hospital occupational therapy instructors from Oakland were moving to Carmel. Dorothy's mother was already living there, and her brother Willard arrived later to start a newspaper called the *Carmel Cymbal*. When the two women arrived in Monterey, they stopped to check on their baggage and missed the connecting stage, so they started walking over the hill to Carmel. Luck was with them and they hitched a ride to the lot in the Fourth Addition that they planned to purchase from Frank Devendorf. That night, their first in Carmel, and against the local rules, they heated soup over a tiny fire in the dirt road and slept on a bed of pine needles. By Friday of their first week, they were inquiring about the water supply to their lot.

"*Rose at 5 after a delightful night's sleep on our pine needles,*" Anne Nash began writing in her diary. "*To the beach to cook our breakfast and then for a long walk by the valley and the woods on the other side. Went to the real estate office . . . but Mr. Devendorf will be back tomorrow. The rest of my baggage came at 3 and we arranged our temporary camp. Heated beans and had a scrumptious dinner.*"

The next day, Devendorf showed them around the undeveloped Fourth Addition, informing them that he doubted he would be able to get water to the lot the two women were most interested in buying, but he would let them know. Anne and

Dorothy began to settle themselves into their camp. During their first week in Carmel, they regularly went to the glistening white sand dunes at the beach where, over an open fire, they cooked breakfasts of scrambled eggs and toast and then lingered over the warming coals before heading to town in search of Devendorf and an answer to their water needs. Each day the question of water went unanswered, but Nash and Bassett were undaunted. They returned to their lot of choice and talked about their house and garden plans before preparing dinner over canned heat.

"A joyous life!" Anne wrote in her diary toward the end of their first week of cooking breakfast at the beach and planning for their new home and garden.

A routine began to set in. For the next few weeks, Nash and Bassett, reluctant to start building a home that didn't have a water supply, went to Devendorf's office to inquire about what progress was being made. Devendorf, sometimes optimistic and sometimes unpromising but always hopeful, said he was trying to see what could be done. The women, anxious to improve on their meager life of camping, found the town dump and salvaged stove parts that they took back to their camp and reassembled.

"Constructed a wonderful stove with rocks as a background—oven and all complete. Dined sumptuously on baked potato, string beans, bacon, and cantaloupe for dessert," Anne noted in her diary.

They went to town to see Devendorf nearly every day, hoping to get some encouragement, innocently unaware that supplying water from the Carmel River to the Fourth Addition was not entirely Devendorf's responsibility. Under the conditions of the sale of Carmel's water plant, it was the responsibility of the Monterey County Water Works to supply water, not only to the developed portions of Carmel but also to the new Fourth Addition. Still, Devendorf was acutely aware of the two women's need for water, so he personally hauled it by horse and cart to their lot. Nash and Bassett at least had some water for their domestic use until Devendorf figured out a more efficient method.

"A beautiful sunny day," Anne wrote in late August. *"(To) town right after breakfast. Met the Marshall on the way who stopped and talked and advised us to build a log cabin . . . Mr. Devendorf not in, hence still no news about the water. Returned to camp and restored our composure by doing a large washing and reading fortifying fragments from Marcus Aurelius. To town again at 3. No mail! No packages. No nothing. Bore this with stoic calmness also. An appetizing dinner . . . and to bed promptly."*

Marcus Aurelius, the Stoic philosopher and emperor of Rome, gave them strength and support while they waited out the question of when, if ever, Carmel River water would arrive at their Fourth Addition lot. At the time, they were unaware that it would be months before water arrived at the Fourth Addition. They also did not know that Devendorf was gradually working on a plan to bring their water entitlement to them. In the meantime, to occupy themselves, Dorothy built a library table. They started a vegetable garden of carrots and a bean patch. They gathered pinecones for their wood stove. They rigged up a lantern and brought books back to camp from the library to read at night. And they read mystery writer Mary Roberts Rinehart, noting, perhaps facetiously, that they found her work humorous. Rinehart had recently published a book titled *The Circular Staircase*, and the first chapter was called "I Take a Summer House." Casting a symbolic message the two women may have readily caught, the book begins:

This is the story of how a middle-aged spinster lost her mind, deserted her domestic gods in the city, took a furnished house for the summer out of town, and found herself involved in one of those mysterious crimes that keep our newspapers and detective agencies happy and prosperous. For twenty years I had been perfectly comfortable; for twenty years I had had the window-boxes filled in the spring, the carpets lifted, the awnings put up and the furniture covered with brown linen; for as many summers I had said good-by to my friends, and, after watching their perspiring hegira, had settled down to a delicious quiet in town where the mail comes three times a day, and the water supply does not depend on a tank on the roof.

And the young women walked down the hill from their lot to look with envy at a house being built. While they waited for news about their much-needed hookup, they grew impatient and increasingly worried about water.

"Sunny and foggy by turns," Anne wrote on August 31, the last day of their first month in Carmel. *"Washed my head and various bits of raiment this morning and enjoyed looking through the books and magazines we had brought from the library at noon. . . . The Marshall called and examined our vegetable beds with interest. . . . Getting more and more worried about building but Mr. Devendorf is out of town."*

The month of September began cloudy, and there was some thunder and lightning. "Suggestions of a storm," Anne called it. They planted scarlet runner beans and some peas and then they sat down and figured out what their expenses had been since they had arrived nearly a month ago. The amount came to $50.26 and included their train fares and freight. As they worried over water, they also began to worry about how long their money would hold out if they couldn't start building their home. Dorothy wondered if they could remain for two more months before they would have to give up their dream. And then, the next day, good news arrived.

"A beautiful sunshiny day!" Anne began her entry for September 2, 1921. *"Worked about all morning chopping wood and getting some beds ready for planting. In between finished 'Hunger'—a strange book. Most realistic. . . . Saw Mr. Devendorf purely by accident and he told us to go ahead with our*

building and that he'd guarantee to get water up here somehow. Said he'd have a man haul enough up in barrels for the actual building if the tank couldn't be installed soon enough. At least we have something definite to work on now, so we will start in."

So Anne and Dorothy set out to realize their plans for a home in Carmel's Fourth Addition. Within a week they met a man who would help them build their house and arrange for an estimate on lumber. The weather held warm, as it's inclined to do at that time of the year, so, contrary to both their parents' advice that it was too late in the year to plant peas, they went ahead and planted peas—and turnips. They took time to read Henry James and, revealingly, they sent a letter to Devendorf telling him they needed employment. A few days later, they traveled to Pacific Grove with their hired carpenter:

Sun by 10 a.m. Mr. Pawley and wife and relatives drove up in their machine just as we had finished breakfast, and took us home with them to Pacific Grove where we stayed to dinner and into the afternoon discussing house plans. Have decided on a high roof and smaller paned windows for the house. Left Pacific Grove at 4:30 to walk back but got picked up by a machine just beyond Monterey. Home a little before 6, rejoiced to see that the farm was undisturbed and that the turnips were up and the peas shooting along. A gorgeous red sunset through the trees.

The next day they formally applied for a water hookup.

September turned stifling hot, by Carmel's standards, as work began on excavating the site and removing large tree roots. They hauled the dirt away in hand buckets until someone loaned them a two-wheel cart. The marshal dropped by, dismounted from his horse, and gave them a hand removing tree roots. At times the heat forced them to retire to some shade. Cost estimates for lumber and plumbing were coming in, and Anne and Dorothy interviewed a woodcutter. Two pines must come down. When the trees were felled, the women felt like they were accomplices to a crime but called it a necessary evil. In the meantime, the late summer hot spell pushed the peas; they were now six inches high. The women ordered gravel to make concrete. They told Devendorf they were going ahead with their building, and he repeated his promise of hauling water to them—even though he knew that, contractually, it was the responsibility of the Monterey County Water Works. Later, a man delivered two huge cans of water sent by Devendorf. At one point, Anne took a break under the shadiest tree she could find and read a collection of the best plays of 1919 and 1920; none impressed this formidable young woman. Toward the end of September, Anne's mother sent them two boxes—one containing a cake and other brown bread, a package of chocolate, a sausage, one orange, and one yellow African marigold.

Actual construction of the house began in October. Anne and Dorothy sawed one-by-twelve sideboards, became "imbued" with the theory of concrete, learned how to plane and nail corner boards, and assisted in putting up rafters and crossbeams. Masons finished the fireplace, putting in a mantle of soapstone. By mid-month the women began shingling the exterior and with Mr. Pawley's help installed two bedroom windows. By early November, Dorothy had finished the roofing.

"Nothing will be hard after slipping about on that precipice," Anne wrote in her diary.

By the middle of November 1921, the house at Alta and Junipero in the Fourth Addition was still unfinished, but Anne and Dorothy broke camp and moved in. Their budget exhausted, the two former occupational therapy instructors from Oakland took odd jobs to meet expenses. They watered, dug ditches, ironed, painted, worked at the post office, and washed dishes. They were now living in their new home, and Devendorf was still hauling water to them by the barrel as he secretly continued to work on his plan to get them a legal water connection from Monterey County Water Works.

In March 1922, with his plan finally in place, Devendorf saw his opportunity. He asked C. S. Olmsted, working for S. F. B. Morse as the Monterey County Water Works superintendent in Pacific Grove, to furnish an estimate for extending a line to the Carmel pumping plant. Olmsted, springing his own trap, said it could be done for $1,488 and then handed the issue over to his company attorney. Devendorf then made the first of two well-calculated risks. First, he consulted with his son-in-law Edward Hohfeld, a partner in the San Francisco law firm of Morrison, Dunne, & Brobeck. They agreed to file a complaint against Morse's Monterey County Water Works with the California Railroad Commission, charging that the water company failed to fulfill its obligation to furnish water to the Fourth Addition. On April 18, Hohfeld had the necessary legal papers ready and mailed them back to Carmel. The packet of legal documents also contained a draft of a letter for the mayor of Carmel to sign. Devendorf had thought it all out. Part of his plan was that his pal Perry Newberry, editor of the *Carmel Pine Cone* and recently elected mayor, would step forward with his political office and influential newspaper behind him and form a united front against the Monterey County Water Works. Newberry went along with Devendorf's plan and no one needed to know otherwise. All Devendorf had to do was wait for the "official" letter from the mayor of Carmel to arrive at his office and he would swing into action. And arrive, it did.

Gentlemen:
It has come to our attention that certain residents and householders in (the) Fourth Addition to Carmel-By-The-Sea have been unable to obtain water service from the Monterey County Water Works, although they have repeatedly requested and demanded such service, and that it has been necessary to haul water at great expense to meet their daily needs; and also that other purchasers from you in said Addition dare not build upon or attempt

to occupy and enjoy their property for fear of inability to obtain water service from said company, although you have, on their behalf, requested and demanded that such service be provided.

As said Fourth Addition lies within the area entitled to water service from the Monterey County Water Works, and the failure of said company to render such service not only works a hardship and injustice upon property owners in that Addition but prevents the normal growth and upbuilding of that part of town and therefore amounts to an injury to all of us, we are of the opinion that prompt and vigorous steps should be taken to compel the furnishing of the service requested, and to that end we hereby offer our fullest cooperation and assistance.

The letter, dated April 22, 1922, was from the office of the mayor of Carmel and was unsigned. It was addressed to the Carmel Development Company, attention Frank Devendorf. As Devendorf read it in his little shingled bungalow real estate office, he knew the impact it would have in his complaint before the California Railroad Commission. As Devendorf had planned, the mayor of Carmel was bringing him both good news and bad news. The letter made it appear that the bad news was that the City of Carmel was getting pressure from some of its waterless and unhappy residents who also happened to be Devendorf's real estate clients. The good news was that Devendorf, who had been hauling water by horse and cart to these same residents, was now going to get the city's support in taking on the powerful Monterey County Water Works, supplier of water from the Carmel River and the legacy of Charles Crocker.

Remarkably and inexplicably, there were three mayors of Carmel in April 1922, two of whom were "short term" and who left office early in the month, and a third, Perry Newberry, who held a newly elected, two-year term. He had just won the mayor's seat on a controlled-growth platform.

Don't Vote for Perry Newberry: If you hope to see Carmel become a city. If you want its growth boosted. If you desire its commercial success. If street lamps on its corners mean happiness to you. If concrete street pavements represent your civic ambitions. If you have less regard for the unique character of Carmel than for the opportunity of money making. If you think a glass factory is of greater value than a sand dune, or a millionaire than an artist, or a mansion than a little brown cottage. If you truly want Carmel to become a boosting, bustling, wide-awake, lively metropolis. Don't Vote For Perry Newberry.

With that brazen and challenging platform, he won the election. He was obviously a man willing to take on any issue affecting the welfare of the townsfolk, including what Newberry saw as an inexcusable absence of water supply to his constituents in the Fourth Addition. With Newberry's "official letter" in hand, Devendorf swung into action. The same day that the letter was sent to the Carmel Development Company, April 22, 1922, he filed a complaint against the Monterey County Water Works, with the California Railroad Commission, alleging that Monterey County Water Works had failed to provide water service to the Fourth Addition.

Unknown to anyone at the time, the letter from Carmel was not written by its mayor. It was composed by Devendorf's son-in-law, attorney Hohfeld, as a scheme to make it appear that the City of Carmel was acting independently in the interests of its waterless residents. The appearance was that Newberry was the antagonist, but in truth, Devendorf was the front man. By April 25, the Railroad Commission of California notified Hohfeld that Devendorf's complaint against the Monterey County Water Works had been received, given a file number, and would get the commission's earliest attention. The complaint noted: "In one case the purchasers of lots in one of said blocks in Fourth Addition have built and are occupying a cottage . . . but have been compelled through failure of said defendant (Monterey County Water Works) to furnish such service, to depend upon water being hauled for their uses."

Dramatically, Devendorf included as an exhibit the map of the Fourth Addition he had outlined in red. On it he had written, "Cottages now occupied. I am hauling water to the parties." And he initialed his own handwriting. He asked the Railroad Commission to order Monterey County Water Works to immediately extend its water system and service to every lot in the Fourth Addition. In early May, attorneys for the Monterey County Water Works responded. They admitted that the company was not serving water to specific lots in the Fourth Addition and further said they would not furnish any water to those lots unless either the Railroad Commission required them to do so or the Carmel Development Company was willing to advance them $1,500 plus 10 percent interest to cover the expansion costs. Monterey County Water Works, they added, would repay the money if the terms of the proposed advance were approved by the Railroad Commission. Besides, they continued to argue, "there is but one family now residing within those blocks and the return from said prospective consumer will amount to approximately $1.50 to $2 a month; that such a return will not begin to equal the operating cost of said extension."

The attorneys were, of course, ignoring the condition in the 1913 sale of the Carmel water plant requiring that Monterey County Water Works supply water to precisely the lots in the Fourth Addition that it was now refusing. The Railroad Commission set a public hearing for Tuesday, June 27, 1922, in Carmel's city hall, domain of Mayor Perry Newberry. The all-too-apparent squeeze was in the making. Within a week after the hearing date had been set, S. F. B. Morse, founder of the Del Monte Properties Company, successor to Charles Crocker's Pacific Improvement Company and president of Monterey County Water Works, surfaced. He acknowledged the 1913 sales agreement and conditions, but instead of pursuing an advance loan of $1,500, he settled for a property exchange between Del Monte Properties and the Carmel Development Company. And he promised to extend the water pipes to the Fourth Addition within sixty days—at his expense. There was one condition. Morse did not want to leave a legal issue hanging on the whim of man or nature: "If we should be delayed in laying our mains in said territory by reason of strikes, labor troubles, acts of God, or other causes over which we have no control, then the time shall be extended during the period of the delay occasioned by any said causes."

The Railroad Commission canceled the hearing that was to be held in Carmel's city hall. Morse, a man of his word, kept it. Devendorf stood by and happily watched as water pipes began stretching out toward the Fourth Addition. On August 8, 1922, Olmsted notified his company's attorney that "the water from the high pressure tanks was turned into the mains yesterday morning, so that everything is in condition to serve Mr. Devendorf's property . . . water is on the premises."

And Anne Nash was back at her diary.

On Wednesday, July 12, 1922, she wrote: "[M]uch excited to see signs of trenches and water pipes (we hope) in our vicinity. Streets signs up, too—making it apparent we are at the corner of Junipero and Alta."

On Friday, July 14, 1922: "[T]he water pipes are going along Alta Avenue, and we have a meter at our boundary in the back!!!"

And then on August 8, 1922: "A year ago today we landed in Carmel and embarked on our unheard of venture! Strange to think of all that has happened since then . . . houses going up, etc., etc. . . . . Another busy afternoon at the P.O. When I got home the hose had already arrived and Dorothy had it running merrily under the oak tree. After dinner (we) worked a bit at the septic tank."

There was an order of dismissal by the Railroad Commission on August 10, 1922.

This saga was not just a symbol of two women's determination, but of the marginal nature of water supply for all the Monterey Peninsula. For Monterey County Water Works, supplying water was an impersonal, commercial, moneymaking venture, its mandate set by Charles Crocker. For Devendorf, the two women were useful pawns in a political power struggle over water from the Carmel River. But it was also a moral issue, a matter of principle, and a pragmatic one, as well. Certainly, water from the Carmel River was not so plentiful by 1921 and 1922 that it arrived easily at the doorsteps of Carmel's new homeowners. Newberry, incidentally, would gather in more fame two years later by suggesting that Carmel install a tollgate, just like Pebble Beach's, and charge motorists coming from Pebble Beach an admission fee to enter Carmel.

It was the plight of Anne Nash and Dorothy Bassett, two single women migrating to Carmel to build their home, which conveniently prompted Newberry's "letter" to Devendorf. The two women were unwilling to wait for their water hookup, so they steadfastly pursued Devendorf as their only way of getting water from the Carmel River. The Fourth Addition was a new expansion, physically elevated above the village's center and located at its northern end. Today locals know they can avoid tourist traffic and reach downtown Carmel via the Fourth Addition by winding their way through a little maze of roads that go right by the tucked-away intersection of Alta and Juniper. It was on Alta that Anne Nash and Dorothy Bassett built their home—and where it stands to this day, complete with a hookup bringing water from the river.

Demand on the river for supplying water to Carmel's Fourth Addition was characteristic of the village—eccentric perhaps, indirect certainly, but effective in the final analysis. It was also characteristic of the population growth hitting the Monterey Peninsula and the expectation new arrivals brought with them that water was a normal part of day-to-day living.

Over the ensuing years, Devendorf's water odyssey was never ending, but he was growing older. By 1934, he was spending more time with his family at their Oakland home. Carmel was growing and thriving in its various eccentric debates and struggles to keep its independent character. Devendorf had also developed Carmel Highlands, five miles to the south of the Carmel River, and water remained its crux. There was a creek running through the Highlands that might solve Devendorf's problems. In late May 1934, he telephoned his right-hand man, Frank DeAmaral, who was later interviewed about that day.

"He called me up and said he was coming out," DeAmaral recalled."He wanted to go up in Wildcat Canyon because there was water up there that he thought we should have. Asked me if I thought I could get a couple of horses and I said, 'Yes, Mr. Devendorf, I can.' So I met him down there with two horses and, of course, I told him before we started, I said, 'We can't ride very far, it's pretty rough. You're not going to go very far on a horse.'" "Well," he said, "we'll go as far as we can."

Wildcat Creek, and its home canyon in the steep coastal heart of the Carmel Highlands, is one of many small streams originating in the Santa Lucia Mountains that make their way uninhibited to the Pacific Ocean, where today they are bridged by the Coast Highway on its way south. In the spring of 1934, the Coast Highway, or U.S. Highway 1, as it is also known, was still under construction south to the Monterey–San Luis Obispo county line. It would be another three years before the ocean-cliff roadway would open to through car traffic and bring motoring tourists to the Monterey Peninsula from the south.

This is desperate country. Each winter heavy torrential rains in the upper backcountry force the coastal edge of the mountain range to cling to its sodden self in a hopeless effort to forestall its inevitable fall into the ocean and the ripping out of huge chunks of the highway on its way down. Homesteaders and early modern-day residents, if they lasted long in this vertical canyon country, learned to watch and listen to the land for signs of when its grip on itself was about to release. In the desperateness of it all, there is an undeniable beauty. On the western slope of the Santa Lucias, the rounded headlands of the mountains seem to sway out into the air. To be there high above the Pacific is like being on a playground swing at its zenith, and from its highest arc on a summer day, you can look out across the ocean and see the silhouette of a freighter, motionless on the horizon. On those perfect days when imagination and light are favorably bent, you can even see the curve of the earth. And God, it can be hot up there. But on any summer afternoon, when nature is in an ironic mood, the fog will draw up those mountain canyons, cooling the sage with its damp air and bursting the brush of its commanding scent of earth and flower before stopping against an invisible wall of heat; and you can walk, full of sweat from the summer's stifling air, into a shoreline of fog for a refreshing breath and then walk out again into the dry parchment of the sun. From up here the Pacific is so far below that not a sound of its waves smashing on granite reaches these slopes. Only the irritating tiny buzz of a fly in the ear or the rush of a hawk's wings pushing itself against the windless sky can be heard.

The land in this vast watershed is so diverse in its magnitude that to come upon a meadow, a small valley, a ridgeline, or canyon creek choked with redwoods for the first time is like entering a new time zone, a world apart from the one just departed. Poets and prose masters have written about this country, as Robinson Jeffers did in his 1920s poem, appropriately titled "The Coast-Road." The poem is about a cowboy on horseback, high on a ridge, looking down at the workers constructing the Coast Highway. He reins up, makes a "gesture of wringing a chicken's neck," and rides higher. The highway below is an unmasked metaphor for the inevitable destruction and the end it will bring to the cowboy's way of life. It is this western slope that is most exposed to the public today as it drives up and down the Coast Highway. This is where Devendorf would make his last stand for water.

"I kept trying to make him stop and come back because I

knew he shouldn't go up there. Something just told me," DeAmaral said.

At the mouth of the little Wildcat, Devendorf struggled to get on his horse; he was older, heavier. He had not been on a horse in a long time. He was semiretired and should have been fully retired, but he couldn't rest knowing that Carmel was barely getting by on a slim margin of water. So he and DeAmaral mounted their horses and began the rocky climb up Wildcat Creek and its canyon. Behind them they could hear the soft padding of the surf as the tide washed little waves ashore. On hot days like this one, the ocean seems to sense the oppression in the windless, hot air and relaxes its relentless mining of the rocky shoreline. On this day there was no coastal fog to cool them as they rode, no breeze reaching into the tight, dark redwood canyon as they climbed higher and higher. No miracles of nature to soothe the heat. At first, an occasional seagull's shriek broke the silence, but the scavengers were staying close to the tidemark and not following the two riders along the drainage that was soaking into the damp creek. Gradually, underfoot and off to the sides of the horses' path, spring wildflowers began to show. Pink one-leaved onions, dingy white stinging phacelias, yellow Pacific silverweeds, and tiny starflowers in the shade of redwoods. Delicate, dew-misted maidenhairs draped down from moist creek banks, deceptive in their tropical incongruity. The canyon with its little ribbon of water grew steeper as they urged the horses upward, leaving the construction of the highway and the change it would bring to the Monterey Peninsula out of sight and hearing far below them.

"And it got so the horses couldn't go any farther. It was just winding over the rocks and all," DeAmaral said. "It was awfully hot."

"Frank, let's tie the horses here," Devendorf said.

They pushed on by foot, climbing over huge boulders, straddling the creek at times, going beyond where the horses could not go.

"Mr. Devendorf, you can't walk up there. That's awfully rough in there," DeAmaral told him. "It was so hot that I as a young fellow was feeling it. And here he was in his late seventies."

"We won't go far."

"So, we come back and he went to town that afternoon. Just one of those things. It had to be. If he hadn't taken that ride, he'd be here a long time. There's a man who had nothing but a kind word."

On Friday, June 3, 1934, Perry Newberry, editor of the *Carmel Pine Cone* and longtime friend and confidant of Devendorf's, ran a small item in his newspaper informing Carmel residents that Devendorf had suffered a heart attack "while here on a business trip." Newberry said the heart attack wasn't as serious as first rumored, that Devendorf was recovering at his Lincoln Street home. The tone of the news article implied that Devendorf was becoming a historic figure, as if the villagers did not know much about him. It was as if Newberry felt obliged to explain who Devendorf was, so many years had passed since he first hauled barrels of water by horse cart to Anne Nash and Dorothy Bassett—and leveraged, with Newberry's surreptitious help, Monterey County Water Works into providing water to the Fourth Addition. Newberry's report was understandably optimistic, but it was premature. Four months after searching for water in Wildcat Canyon, Devendorf was driven by ambulance back to his Oakland home and family, where he died on October 9, 1934. He was seventy-eight. The business trip Newberry referred to, of course, was about water—simply an old antagonist that would never go away. Years later, DeAmaral went back to Wildcat Canyon, this time not to look for water but in search of a suitable boulder for mounting a sculpture of Devendorf. The sculpture was made by Devendorf's oldest daughter, Edwina. The memorial was placed in a corner of Carmel's downtown Devendorf Park by another of his daughters, Lillian (Mrs. Edward Hohfeld), and her daughter, Devendorf's granddaughter, Jane Hohfeld Galante.

"The weather hasn't been kind to the bronze," Jane said. "It has become streaked, making my grandfather look rather sour, and he wasn't."

Devendorf may well have been naïve to go into Carmel Highlands, not just to build there but to look for water. He was not an engineer. He sold real estate, resolved minor disputes, and helped newcomers with their daily problems. Other than convincing the Monterey County Water Works that it should fulfill its legal obligation, water supply from the Carmel River was a relatively simple matter in the early years of Carmel's' development. But it got more complicated as time wore on. Yes, the Carmel Development Company bought and sold water rights and drilled wells to supplement its supply and meet its growing demand. Unlike the Pacific Improvement Company, however, the Carmel Development Company was not in the water business nor was it a developer demanding water that it could not produce. There were no demands by the Carmel Development Company for another dam, larger reservoirs, or more pipelines. The demand, in good conscience, was on Devendorf to find it, not create it. Today, there are no pioneers like Anne Nash and Dorothy Bassett. There is no community of artists, writers, professors, and intelligentsia in Carmel—as Devendorf envisioned. Artists and scholars are splintered, unable to afford a home there, living on the outskirts, while Carmel thrives on its heritage as an artists' colony. Still, there remains an undeniable demand for water. That demand meant a third dam on the Carmel River.

7 〰 SARDINES AND GOLF COURSES

Yet Another Dam

Who, other than possibly Charles Crocker, back in 1880, ever dreamed that by the middle of the twentieth century the Monterey Peninsula would be so utterly and completely dependent on a singular source of water of such modest means as the Carmel River? The answer to that question is that Crocker's successors knew what the future held as long as they controlled the river. S. F. B. Morse, often considered a visionary by his followers, knew because his Del Monte Properties Company owned vast water rights to the Carmel River and much of the land along its banks. Owners of private-interest water companies such as the Monterey County Water Works and its successor, California Water and Telephone Company, knew what the future held because of their unhampered capability to build dams on the river.

Obviously, the two powers are often one and the same or share common interests. The water purveyors were confident that if a dam became obsolete, the easiest and most immediate solution to solving water shortage problems on the Monterey Peninsula was to build another dam on the river. This was especially true when the San Clemente Dam, thought to have a thirty-year longevity when built in 1921, started showing signs of being incapable of meeting growth demands in 1948—twenty-seven years after it began storing river water. All it took to meet the Monterey Peninsula's growing needs for water, in addition to the San Clemente, was another dam—this time the Los Padres Dam, in 1949. Revealingly, engineers working on the Los Padres project publicly predicted that it would only be sufficient for twenty years. If water-company engineers knew the life span of a particular dam, then it only follows that when needed, they could build another dam on the Carmel River to meet the water requirements of a growing population and such blossoming industries as sardine fishing, golf courses, tourism, and highly attractive spectator events. Comfortable with the knowledge or confidence that a dam was always in its future, the Monterey Peninsula took every opportunity to reinvent itself when a new public relations image was in its best interests. In one era it became the "Sardine Capital of the World," in a later era the "Golf Capital of the World." Regardless of the region's economic base, the Monterey Peninsula remains dependent on water from the Carmel River and to get that additional water it is dependent on dams.

Ultimately, the San Clemente Dam and its reservoir did not capture and contain enough water to meet the growing population of the Monterey Peninsula. The demand for water from the Carmel River not only came from the Hotel Del Monte, and its systematic development of towns like Monterey and Pacific Grove, but from a burgeoning sardine (pilchard) industry that would grow to sixteen water-consuming canneries and fourteen reduction plants on Cannery Row, and later from resort and public golf courses. What the diverse industries had in common was that all needed copious amounts of water from the Carmel River to maintain themselves. Monterey's sardine industry was the first large-scale commercial user of Carmel River water as the canneries steadily increased production each year in the decade following World War I. Average production in tonnage of sardines for the ten years after World War I was forty-three tons per year. During the decade of the Great Depression, tonnage increased to 155 tons per year. In 1938 sardines became an eight-million-dollar industry. That year there were more than fifty purse-seine boats in the Monterey fleet, each with a twelve-man crew supplying sardines to twenty-five hundred cannery workers. Together they were Monterey's largest, single workforce. Roughly 30 percent of Monterey's population was either directly employed by the fishing industry or in an indirect but related manner. The sardine industry hit its stride in World War II with the military's need for canned foods that could be easily stored and supplied to the troops. The 1941–42 season was the highest, most profitable year on record at the time. Even though many of the fishing boats were used for government defense work, such as coastal patrols, the fleet managed to haul in a tremendous 249,717 tons. The next two seasons were nearly as good, and Sicilian fishermen and their first-generation descendents were making large group investments in U.S. savings bonds. The nutritional sardine became a basic wartime food, and the Monterey Peninsula began calling itself "The Sardine Capital of the World," even though it was actually third in world production behind ports in Norway and England.

The canneries operated around the clock. Monterey had never seen such a booming business. One cannery boasted that the average time it took a sardine to reach market was "four hours from the boat to labeled can." When the fishing boats arrived offshore, the canneries signaled their workers with shrill whistle calls. Each cannery had its own signal to notify its workers, and the whistles, symbolic of Monterey's new prosperity, blew at any time of the day or night. Noncannery workers complained that the whistles disturbed their sleep, and gradually the canneries started using the telephone to call in their employees. After that, the only time it was obvious that the canneries were in production was when the wind carried a distinctive odor across Monterey. Because of this odor, Monterey became known as "Monterey-by-the-Smell." Following suit, nearby Pacific Grove, because of its Methodist influence, became "Pacific Grove-by-God," and Carmel was simply "Carmel-by-the-Sea."

During their intense production process, the canneries and their satellite reduction plants were dependent on a combination of salt water pumped from the bay and freshwater piped from the Carmel River. The sardines were kept in salt water as they went up the fish ladders and into the first holding tanks. Freshwater from the river was used in the second-stage holding tanks where the sardines' heads, tails, and offal were removed. Water from the river was again used to create steam in both the canning and reduction plants for the "can washer." All the cans were washed with freshwater before they went into the "retort" or large ovens where the sardines were steam cooked. The canneries' demand for water from the Carmel River was so great that by May 1945, construction was underway on an eighteen-inch pipeline able to deliver twenty million gallons of water a day from the river to the canneries. Once in place, in 1946, the pipeline bypassed the existing domestic water main, thus restoring water pressure for homes and the city's firefighting equipment and presumably alleviating the "summer sickness" that struck infants and young children during dry seasons because of poor water quality.

Ten months after the pipeline construction had actually started, the California Water and Telephone Company, owner of the water system, made the project official. On February 8, 1946, the company published a notice that construction of a pipeline carrying water from the river to the canneries was underway and the only reason the $400,000 project had not started earlier was because it was "delayed while our country was at war." The new pipeline taking water from the Carmel River to the canneries was also intended to meet the "exceptional growth on the Peninsula which occurred from 1940 to date." The mains were sterilized and a filter plant installed during the construction period to "assure uniformly clear sparkling water." Halfway down the list of six itemized subjects, the company revealed a large-scale plan for taking even more water from the river with this declaration: "Foundation exploration and design studies for a new dam to be constructed when water requirements on the Peninsula warrant. This has been in progress for some time and will be continued extensively during this year."

Absent any need for regulatory or pubic involvement, the company's announcement was matter-of-fact. When the water company—and only the water company—deemed a new dam on the river was necessary, then the water company would build it. Although a date for construction of another dam was not included in the proclamation, it soon became evident that a new dam across the Carmel River was actually in the company's immediate plans.

World War II drew to an end and coincidentally so did the sardine fishing industry. The glory years when limitless sardines were offloaded at Cannery Row were about over. The 1946–47 season brought in only 26,818 tons of sardines. The abrupt decline had nothing to do with the end of World War II, when the slogan was "Unless You Pack It Our Boys Can't Eat It." The large schools of sardines in Monterey Bay literally disappeared and no one agreed on what happened to them. "The sardines were fished out of the bay," people argued. "All the sardines went into cans, that's where they went." Others argued the opposite. "No, the sardines went someplace else. They didn't like the water here, that's what happened to them." Or as one fisherman said after returning with empty holds, "It seemed like a change of water or current. All the fish seemed to vanish at once."

While the debate escalated, the California Water and Telephone Company and its supporters, oblivious to the potential consequences of losing a major industry, continued to argue for a larger pipeline to bring water from the river to the sardine canneries, and continued their planning for another dam on the Carmel River. Ignoring the highly publicized dispute over what happened to the sardine made it easier to rationalize that the need for water was in fact to support population growth.

Although the sardine disappeared overnight, the calls for conservation of the fish came as early as 1941 when Edwin L. Carty, California's fish and game commissioner, advocated that a sufficient number of fish be allowed to escape the fishing nets so they could spawn and reproduce in larger numbers. He warned that the elimination of the large sardine would curtail reproduction. That same year Frances H. Clark, of the California Department of Fish and Game, wrote a newspaper article in which he argued that the sardine could not withstand the vast exploitation by the industry. He outlined a five-point conservation program for the fishing industry and canners to follow. He suggested curtailment of the present catch, building up the supply by smaller catches, holding the total take at the maximum level of production, abolishing permits for straight reduction of the sardine, and, most important of all, he asked for sacrifices to be made by the entire industry. None of these suggestions was adopted in whole or part by the industry or the state for another seven years, but by that time the fish had virtually disappeared and the industry had collapsed.

One of the most persistent and articulate experts on the sardine was Edward F. Ricketts of the Pacific Biological Lab on Cannery Row and immortalized as "Doc" in John Steinbeck's *Cannery Row*. Describing, in 1947, how the fish feed on microscopic plants, Ricketts wrote,

When water temperatures were low and unfavorable to fish, as in 1941 and 1942, care should have been taken not to reduce breeding stock. Instead, each year the number of canneries increased. Each year we expended more fishing energy pursuing fewer fish. Until in the 1944-46 seasons we reached the peak of the effort, but with fewer and fewer results. Each year we've been digging a little further into the breeding stock. The answer to the question "Where are the sardines?" becomes quite obvious. . . . They're in the cans. The parents of the sardines we need so badly now were being ground up into fishmeal, were extracted for oil, were being canned, too many of them, far too many. A really good year will be an evil thing for the industry. And still worse for Monterey. Because we'll forget our fears of the moment, queer misguided mortals that .

we are! We'll disregard conservation proposals as we have in the past; we'll sabotage those already enacted. And the next time this happens we'll really be sunk. Monterey will have lost its chief industry. And this time for good!

John Steinbeck, in early January 1963, less than a month after being awarded the Nobel Prize for Literature, reflected on the earlier period when he and his friend Ricketts tried to save the sardine. He wrote,

> The canneries were warned again and again that they were destroying the species. There was even an act of the legislature limiting the catch until it was removed during the war. It is no mystery why the fish disappeared. They were hunted for at sea, hunted by aircraft and taken in such numbers that the schools could not restore themselves. Both Ed Ricketts and I wrote impassioned pleas to the industry to get them to limit the catch, but they wouldn't do it. And so, they lost the canneries. It's a shame, but they wanted the buck. I guess we all must learn.

The sardine industry was slow to learn and deaf to warnings that the fish could never rebound under the fishing pressure of the 1940s. As Ricketts, Steinbeck, and the other experts pointed to scientific facts in their effort to save the fish, Monterey's sardine industry was not only looking forward to a new and exclusive pipeline from the Carmel River, it was also busy seeking permits from the California Fish and Game Commission for nine more canning plants that would never be built.

Looking back to 1946, when the California Water and Telephone Company made its belated announcement that it was installing a pipeline that would bring water from the Carmel River to Monterey's canneries, it appears that the company's real purpose was to raise public awareness that another dam was going to be built on the river—even though there was no apparent need for public approval. Like the corporate tone of many annual reports, it was a matter of persuading a "shareholding" public that growth, whether commercial or residential, was a good thing, and for it to continue, another dam had to be added to the Carmel River. The water company was coming to the rescue and its timing couldn't have been better. Less than two months earlier, on December 10, 1945, in a letter to the editor of the *Monterey Peninsula Herald*, S. F. B. Morse set in motion public thinking that another dam was the best thing for the Monterey Peninsula. Morse, whose Del Monte Properties Company formerly owned the predecessor to the California Water and Telephone Company, claimed he had no interest in California Water and Telephone's intentions other than being a water consumer, but he wrote,

> The water company (California Water and Telephone) owns another reservoir site immediately adjoining the existing one. It is of approximately the same size as the present reservoir. It is a most excellent dam site and there is no problem involved whatsoever in its construction . . . Any time [*sic*], however, that additional storage is necessary the water company owns a dam site and part of the land in a reservoir so large that it will be greater than the capacity of the other two mentioned by perhaps thrice times. . . . The Del Monte Properties Company, of which the writer is president, used to own and operate the Monterey County Water Works. It built the present dam and reservoir. It has no interest whatsoever, direct or indirect, in the company that now owns the water system except as a consumer of water.

Contrary to his disclaimer, as a commercial consumer of water, Morse's company clearly stood to benefit from a new dam. In fact, the Del Monte Properties Company had always been in a favorable position when it came to using water from the Carmel River. For example, when Morse sold Monterey

County Water Works to California Water and Telephone Company in 1930, the deal included an agreement that his company retained the right to receive up to 35 percent of the flow of the Carmel River and to receive this water at a preferred rate—a key provision in the sale that went undisclosed until 1958. In effect, this meant that the people of the Monterey Peninsula unknowingly subsidized Morse's private use of water, including the irrigation of his golf courses. So a new dam was an easy and welcome proposition for Morse. It would guarantee more water from the Carmel River for his company's resort properties and its future golf courses, and assured a continued flow of water to the Hotel Del Monte, which was now being touted as a site for a U.S. Naval postgraduate school. In fact, Morse sold the hotel and grounds in 1948 to the U.S. Navy, less than two years after he wrote his letter. As for his insider information, comforting the public that there was an even larger reservoir site for still another dam when the time came, Morse withheld the identity of the location for another two months. Then, on February 15, 1946, in a follow-up news article headlined, "Morse Statement Clarifies Peninsula Water Situation," Morse revealed that a dam could be built at Syndicate Camp, a private campground on the Carmel River dating back to 1889. In a matter-of-fact manner, he said that a dam at this site would flood the entire Cachagua Valley because of its downstream location. Cachagua Valley was a sparsely populated region favored by people who sought their privacy, by anglers, and by deer hunters. He also stated in the article that the proposed Los Padres Dam, upriver from the Cachagua Valley, would not only be inexpensive to build, "it will take care of the requirements of this region, in my estimation, for twenty-five or thirty years, and it is possible that it will take care of it for all time because the Peninsula is limited in area."

Carmel Valley farmers relying on water from the river were far from agreeing with Morse's proclamation that water from the Carmel River might supply the needs of the Monterey Peninsula into infinity. In September 1947, while the upper end of

Carmel Valley was being subdivided into small homesites, lower Carmel Valley remained predominately pear orchards and cover crops. The farmers blamed a lack of rainfall, increased water use from the river, and new wells pumping large quantities of water from the riverbed for shrinking the level of the river and its underground water table. They predicted the eventual loss of their orchards and crops if more water from the river was diverted into direct pipelines running through the valley to the developing urban areas of the Monterey Peninsula. During the fall of 1947, the surface of the river was dry, no water was flowing in the Carmel River, but there was enough water moving underground to supply both private and water-company pumps throughout the valley, according to the news article. Water company officials admitted that the reservoir at San Clemente Dam was low, but argued it had been low before. As for pumping water from wells in the river, the company said that daily use of its six wells accounted for only 19 percent of all the water used on the Monterey Peninsula, and those wells did not pose a threat to the underground water used by the farmers. As far as the water company was concerned, there was no water shortage on the Monterey Peninsula or in Carmel Valley. "The river will be an adequate water supply for many years to come," countered Pete A. Nenzel, vice president of California Water and Telephone Company, based in San Francisco.

On October 3, 1947, a month after the farmers sounded the alarm, and only nine months after California Water and Telephone Company first announced it was studying the prospects of another dam on the Carmel River, a short news article appeared in the *Monterey Peninsula Herald* reporting that the water company was actually going to build a dam that would "extend straight across the Carmel River and will consist of non-penetrable dirt and crushed rock." Apparently, residents of the Monterey Peninsula had been prepared for the announcement. The news that another dam would be built on the Carmel River had about as much impact on the public as a raindrop hitting a hot sidewalk. It instantly evaporated. Morse was prophetic when he predicted, "There is no problem involved whatsoever in its construction." The only mention of concern at the time was a paragraph in the same news item: "Valley residents, learning of the type of dam contemplated, already have expressed fears the new dam might 'break' and flood the Cachagua area and even the Carmel Valley itself." C. M. Goldsworthy, local manager for California Water and Telephone Company, dismissed those concerns saying that the dam had to have approval of the state of California and, like school buildings, it had to meet earthquake construction standards. There was no prolonged environmental impact study, no series of public hearings debating the feasibility of a dam on the river. Apparently the lone safeguard at the time was an inspector from the State Division of Water Resources, who came to the construction site about every ten days.

In early May 1948, Goldsworthy announced that the Macco Corporation, which had recently completed a large landfill project at the San Francisco International Airport, had been awarded the $848,000 contract to construct Los Padres Dam. Sited six miles upstream of the San Clemente Dam, the earth-filled Los Padres was engineered to store 3,300 acre feet, or twice the reservoir size of the San Clemente, with a spillway capacity of 23,000 cubic feet per second. Work would begin within the week and was expected to be completed in eight months—all contingent on the state's approval of the plans. When finished, the reservoir would triple the amount of water storage for the Monterey Peninsula.

"Monterey Peninsula's new dam, bridging its canyon in the remote Santa Lucia mountains, will provide a strong link in the lifeline of utilities serving local communities and their development far into the future," a reporter for the *Monterey Peninsula Herald* noted with editorial zeal, echoing the days of the local newspaper support for Charles Crocker.

Immediately, large earth-moving equipment arrived at Barnes Flat, where the dam was to be erected, and the first cadre of workers, about ninety of an eventual two hundred, began arriving at the work site. Prince's Camp, where they would be housed and fed, began to take on the look of a small boomtown as trailers, Quonset huts, and mess halls sprang up. As work began on the foundation of the dam, workers also started replacing the old transmission pipes to the Monterey Peninsula with thirty-six-inch lines. Ironically, by the time the dam, twice the length of a football field, was finished in late December 1948, three weeks behind schedule, the sardines had vanished from Monterey Bay, and the canneries and their accompanying reduction plants were no longer in need of the volumes of river water they required just a few years earlier.

As the sardine fishing industry and its demand for river water was going into a fatal dive, a new leisure industry that would use even more water from the Carmel River was beginning to emerge. When the sardine fishing was at its height, it provided employment only from August to about mid-February each year. Monterey needed more than seasonal employment, it needed a stable year-round economy. Merchants were desperate for more winter business. The local business community decided that a special event bringing spectators by the thousands to the Monterey Peninsula was the answer. So in the spring of 1946, Ted Durein, a young sports writer at the *Monterey Peninsula Herald*, wrote a letter to Bing Crosby asking if the famous singer might be interested in moving the golf tournament he had started in Southern California before World War II to the Monterey Peninsula. Crosby replied yes. There were some informal organizational meetings and on January 11, 1947, less than a year after Durein's letter, Crosby arrived with his entourage of seventy-five professional golfers and their colorful celebrity partners. That was the beginning of today's AT&T Pebble Beach National Pro-Am. It was also the beginning of a tradition of large spectator events on the Monterey Peninsula that would each require volumes of water from the Carmel River. In 1947, two years before Los Padres Dam, there were just five golf courses on the Monterey Peninsula. All five were built either by Crocker's original Pacific Improvement Company or by its successor, Morse's Del Monte Properties Company, and all were dependent on the Carmel River for irrigation water. Their ancestry and dependence on the river can be traced directly to the Hotel Del Monte. Effectively waiting in the wings was a new industry, one built not on labor but on leisure—and that was the golf course. The sardine industry was the first large commercial user of water from the Carmel River; the golf course industry was to be the next.

Some historical background is necessary to understand the proliferation of golf courses on the Monterey Peninsula and the vast quantities of freshwater that golf courses drew from the Carmel River following the building of Los Padres Dam.

The Pacific Improvement Company built an eighteen-hole golf course in 1897. The course was among the first west of the hundredth meridian, the longitudinal boundary dividing the moister East from the arid West. To compound what would seem to be an insurmountable water supply problem, the golf course was not only west of the hundredth meridian it was also on the far western edge of unpredictably water-short California. Other than meager seasonal rainfall, there was no watering system for the new golf course's fairways, and the putting greens were actually hard-packed sand. To give the greens a smooth putting surface, light fuel oil or a similar substance was commonly used. However, the lack of adequate rain was not an obstacle when the time came to convert the golf course from a dry hard-packed surface to a comparative tropical dampness. Under the legal concept of "beneficial use," irrigation water was available from the Carmel River. Within a year or so after taking over the Pacific Improvement Company's Monterey Peninsula holdings, in 1915, eastern-bred Morse applied his firsthand experience in irrigation, gained from his days in the San Joaquin Valley. First he ran a pipeline to the golf course and installed a sprinkling system for the fairways. Then he replaced the sand greens with turf and began watering them. The conversion from a dry golf course typical of an arid West to a well-watered course more typical of the East set a trend for golf-course lushness that continues throughout the West today. Now the Del Monte Golf Course is touted by its corporate publicists as being the first in the world to have green fairways throughout the year. In a more rational golf world, this is not as notable as it may sound. There are many golf courses in the world that either for economical reasons or environmental constraints—because of water shortages—or both, choose not to have year-round green fairways. But once again, the perpetual motion of Crocker's legacy of continuous development dependent on water from the Carmel River, advanced by advertising and publicity campaigns, was unstoppable. Throughout the early twentieth century, no one was interested in stopping it or even slowing it down. Progress was coming to paradise.

Twenty-two years after the opening of the Del Monte Golf Course, Pebble Beach Golf Links followed, in 1919. Then came the Monterey Peninsula Country Club, in 1926, and Cypress Point Club, in 1928. These three golf courses—virtually exclusive to the wealthy, the politically connected, or corporate expense accounts—are all located on the pipeline that Chinese workers installed in 1883, a pipeline that extended from the rock-stone dam built at the junction of San Clemente Creek and the Carmel River, a pipeline that leads directly to the Hotel Del Monte and its original golf course. With the exception of the World War II years, golf courses have been built on the Monterey Peninsula in every decade of the twentieth century.

Today there are twenty golf courses, and the Monterey Peninsula markets itself as the "Golf Capital of the World," even though there are regions in the world with a far greater concentration of courses. Some golf courses are part of real estate communities, such as the Pebble Beach enclave, Carmel Valley Ranch, and Quail Lodge, the latter two bordering the river. The majority of golf courses on the Monterey Peninsula either are private clubs not open to the general public or are high-end resorts.

Of the twenty golf courses on the Monterey Peninsula, fourteen receive either all or part of their water from the river or its aquifer—it's important to note that the California State Water Resources Control Board does not make a distinction between Carmel River water and groundwater in the river's alluvial aquifer or subterranean stream. There are four golf courses actually bordering the banks of the river—two at public Rancho Canada and one each at Carmel Valley Ranch Resort and The Golf Club at Quail Lodge, which are both private. Combined, these four golf courses are among the largest extractors of water from the river's aquifer, second only to the California-American Water Company (Cal-Am) with its forty thousand connections serving an estimated one hundred thousand customers.

In the 1990s, year by year, in both drought years and extremely wet years, these four golf courses, pumping from a total of eleven wells, took a total of 8,461.06 acre feet of water from the aquifer beneath the Carmel River. That totals more than 2.7 billion gallons of water extracted from the Carmel River by four golf courses between 1990 and 1999. Another way to look at this water consumption is to calculate the average amount of water used by each of the four courses on a daily basis during the decade of the 1990s. That figure averages 188,838 gallons of water per day for each golf course on the river. To break it down further, that's 7,868 gallons per hour, twenty-four hours a day, for each golf course. Water extraction from the river does not end with these four courses, however. Ten golf courses on the Monterey Peninsula rely on Carmel River water via Cal-Am's pipeline. This number includes all eight golf courses within the Pebble Beach confines known as Del Monte Forest: Pebble Beach Golf Links, The Links at Spanish Bay, two courses at Monterey Peninsula Country Club, Peter

Hay (a par-three course), Cypress Point Club, Spyglass Hill, and Poppy Hills. Only Poppy Hills is open to the public. All the others are either private or resort golf courses. Other golf courses outside the terrain of Pebble Beach but also on the Cal-Am pipeline are Pacific Grove Golf Course, a public facility, and Old Del Monte. The amount of river water these courses use is significantly less than the four in Carmel Valley. One reason for this is the difference in climate zone between golf courses nearer the coast and those just a few miles inland. Summer temperatures can be fifteen degrees higher in Carmel Valley, requiring more water to keep the courses in competitive lushness with the coastal courses.

The ten golf courses using Cal-Am river water during the same 1990s period as the four in Carmel Valley began the decade by consuming just over 1,000 acre feet of river water between them—compared to the 1,587 acre feet that was pumped from the river by the four Carmel Valley courses. But even this combined consumption of 1,000 acre feet took a big dip in 1994 when eight of the ten golf courses changed their water-use habits and reduced their thirst.

To mitigate its use of river water, the Pebble Beach Company, which does not have its own wells, in October 1994 began a reclamation project to use wastewater for irrigating the eight golf courses within Del Monte Forest. The project was in cooperation with the Monterey Peninsula Water Management District (MPWMD), Carmel Area Wastewater District, and Pebble Beach Community Services District. The company's reasoning for using wastewater is that it reduces the amount of potable water the golf courses use for irrigation. Data from the MPWMD proves the company correct. The first year wastewater was used on the golf courses in Pebble Beach, the total consumption of river water—for all ten courses, including the two not using reclaimed wastewater—dropped to 814 acre feet. The next year usage was down to 466 acre feet. It jumped back to 726 acre feet in 1996 and then settled into a steady decline by the end of the 1990s decade. Overall, the ten courses achieved a nearly 50 percent reduction in their use of water from the Carmel River in the final six years of the 1990s, using an average of 4.24 percent of all water drawn from the river. During the same period of decline in water consumption by the ten golf courses, Cal-Am's residential customers, numbering close to one hundred thousand, were making virtually no progress in reducing their use of the river's water. Requiring an average of 45 percent of all water drawn from the river, homeowners began the 1990s using 6,128 acre feet (1992) and ended the 1990s using 7,180 acre feet (1999), for an average of 7,128 acre feet per year.

While the Pebble Beach Company's use of reclaimed wastewater was a notable goodwill effort, by 2008 there was a hitch still unresolved: reclaimed wastewater is "hot" or heavy in salts, which can burn the grass. To counter this potential damage, Carmel River water is used on a periodic schedule to "flush" the greens and fairways. This flushing has taken place four to six times a year since the project began in 1994. Depending on the actual flow of the river, combined with community demand, the drawdown from flushing can have a potentially severe impact on the river. Examples of "community demand" are major spectator events like the AT&T Pebble Beach National Pro-Am Golf Tournament each February, various car and motorcycles races at the Laguna Seca track, beginning in May, the Monterey Bay Blues Festival in June, and the Monterey Jazz Festival in September. When river flow is threatened during these high-demand periods, combined with the flushing of the golf-course greens and fairways, the steelhead in the river are also threatened. To make matters worse, the impact of a serious drawdown is compounded when the river is in "dry back." Kevan Urquhart, senior fisheries biologist for the MPWMD, explains it this way.

"As river flows decrease naturally in the spring and summer, they can no longer compensate for the draw of the riparian wells that are used every year to extract water from the lower Carmel Valley to serve the community, so the river dries back upstream.

"If the pumping rate is increased or additional wells are put into service to meet demand for freshwater to flush the golf course greens and fairways for accumulated salts and minerals, then it will increase the rate that the river dries back.

"Increased community demand on the Cal-Am system during hot weather, including that caused by large community events that draw many visitors to the peninsula, short seven-day cycles of increased diversion to flush Pebble Beach golf course greens and fairways, and increased temperatures stimulating evapotranspiration of streamside vegetation along the whole river corridor, all can accelerate the rate at which the river dries back in the spring and summer."

If golf-course greens are flushed at a time when the river is drying back, accelerating dewatering of the Carmel River, employees are sent out by the MPWMD to rescue the fish by moving them upstream into areas expected to sustain flowing water year-round, or into the Sleepy Hollow Steelhead Rearing Facility. Regular steelhead rescues are conducted every year as part of an ongoing mitigation program required by the California Environmental Quality Act to lessen the impact of all the various diversions that exist to meet community water demand, including the flushing of golf-course greens. To its credit, the Pebble Beach Company has skipped or delayed flushing to avoid environmental conflicts involving the river, according to Urquhart. To offset the threat to the fish and reduce its use of Carmel River water, the company rebuilt its old Forest Lake Reservoir to hold 105 million gallons of recycled water and installed a micro-filtration reverse-filtration system in 2005–6 at an estimated cost of $10.9 million. Treated water is pumped to the reservoir from a sewage treatment plant near the mouth of the Carmel River. This filtration application is commonly used in filtering liquids and separating bacteria from water. If the filtration system meets water quality standards, the use of Carmel River water for flushing golf courses in Pebble Beach will end—with one caveat: the company retains the legal right in perpetuity to use river water for flushing its golf courses, according to the Monterey Peninsula Water Management District. The Pebble Beach Company is financing the project through the sale of water entitlements to residential users within Del Monte Forest—the entitlements obtained by the company's guarantee to underwrite the first phase of the work.

As a footnote to flushing the golf-course greens, the MPWMD reports that "in recent years, Pebble Beach Community Service District only used treated river water from Carmel Area Wastewater District for the golf courses when they were flushing the greens up to six times a year." For the first time ever, they did not flush the greens at all in water year 2010, which is October 2009 through September 2010. The Community Service District is not expected to flush the golf-course greens with Carmel River water in the foreseeable future unless the Carmel Area Wastewater District's microfiltration/reverse-osmosis process feeding water to Forest Lake fails to meet water quality objectives in the future.

"With the new microfiltration/reverse-osmosis enhancements to the tertiary-treated water produced by the Carmel Area Wastewater District, Forest Lake in Pebble Beach can be filled with recycled water good enough that they don't have to flush the greens with river water any more. Legally they can do so at any time in the future that the MF/RO-tertiary-treated Carmel Area Wastewater District water fails to meet the water quality criteria in their contract for recycled water, but so far, so good," Urquhart said.

8 ⟨⟨⟨ THE ERA OF DISRESPECT

An Environmental Awakening

The golf courses' reliance on water from the Carmel River only exacerbated what would be an ongoing problem of meeting the water requirements of a continually escalating population. Eventually it became apparent to Cal-Am that the building of the Los Padres Dam in 1949 was not a permanent solution to solving the increasing water demands of the Monterey Peninsula. In the thinking of the time, the obvious solution to providing water—not only to the burgeoning golf courses but also to a residential and transient demand—was to build still another dam on the river. And in 1970, that's what the California-American Water Company (Cal-Am) set out to do.

In 1959 the state legislature adopted the California Water Plan devised by the California Department of Water Resources. This plan projected a series of dams, reservoirs, aqueducts, canals, and pipelines stretching the length of the state to meet growing demands for more water and flood control. In 1960 voters statewide approved a $1.75-billion bond issue, giving the California Department of Water Resources a mandate to build a water-producing infrastructure throughout the state. Passage of the bonds signaled to water purveyors, both private and public, that there would be no objection from the public sector when the time came to fulfill the California Water Plan's objectives. It was the public's mood at the time. Throughout the 1960s and '70s, dams, canals, terminal reservoirs, and pumping plants were either under construction or completed. In 1968 the California Aqueduct was inching its way down the San Joaquin Valley heading for Southern California.

During this boom period, the Los Padres Dam fulfilled the prediction that its life span would be only twenty years. Like San Clemente Dam before it, the Los Padres Dam and its reservoir did not, could not, keep up with the Monterey Peninsula's thirst for water. An increasing population, more golf courses, tourism—accompanied by an emerging leisure industry centered on special events—all wanted their share of water, whatever that share might be, from the Carmel River. Not surprisingly, considering the California Water Plan mandate and the dam-building tradition of past water companies, Cal-Am, the latest in a succession of water-company owners controlling the river, automatically declared it was going to build still another dam on the river. The year, again, was 1970, and the location was downstream from the Los Padres Dam in the Cachagua Valley.

The water company's announcement was a chilling reminder of S. F. B. Morse's foresight twenty-five years earlier, when he wrote that there was land "in a reservoir so large that it will be greater than the capacity of the other two . . . by perhaps thrice times." The remote Cachagua Valley is parallel to the larger Carmel Valley immediately to the north, and the Carmel River passes through it before entering the Carmel Valley on its way to the sea. It's a region socially and geographically unto itself and for years has been zealously guarded by its few—fiercely independent—residents. Pulitzer Prize–winning playwright and local resident Martin Flavin once wrote of the Cachagua, "The tiny valley has a name, but I will not name it for you. You can find it for yourself if you feel so inclined, but I rather hope you won't. I do not court publicity for it, I have nothing to sell." The title of his piece was "The Forthright Opinions of an Anti-Suburbanite."

Cal-Am's proposed dam would flood Flavin's Cachagua Valley, just as Morse said it would. Contrary to the statewide pro-dam climate created by the 1959 California Water Plan, people living in the Cachagua were stunned that the water company would inundate their valley, much like North Sacramento Valley's Whiskeytown when it went under water in 1963. Whiskeytown, Oak Bottom, and Grizzly Gulch were late 1880s mining camps, and when construction of a dam on Clear Creek began in 1959, about two hundred people were still living there. Their property was purchased, a cemetery relocated, and the Whiskeytown post office and store moved to higher ground to make way for a reservoir that would cover the historic area with 241,100 acre feet of water, now called the Whiskeytown National Recreational Area. Cachagua residents, unimpressed with the California Water Plan, immediately formed a small opposition force.

"All I can tell you now is that the whole Cachagua Valley is so darned upset that it's in a state of shock," famous cowboy artist and Cachagua rancher Jack Swanson was quoted in the *Monterey Peninsula Herald*. "There are two hundred people here whose lives would be affected."

Cachagua property owners met at the home of Sean Flavin, lawyer son of playwright Martin Flavin. A fact-finding committee was appointed. It included Swanson, Brad Tomasini, Mike Hughes, John Sigourney, and Jane Hohfeld Galante, granddaughter of Carmel's cofounder Frank Devendorf. Although few in numbers, their strategy was to attract sympathy and support from outside the sparsely populated Cachagua Valley. They did this with an indirect but novel approach—they made posters. The message on the posters was a simple one. It read, "Help us to protect your right to enjoy this environment, write your supervisor or representative, sign a petition." There wasn't even the mention of a proposed dam, but there was the word "inundation" and that was enough.

The next year, 1971, Cal-Am dropped its plan to flood Cachagua with a dam and reservoir and instead said it would build a forty-thousand-acre-foot "Super San Clemente Dam" downstream. That dam never materialized because the U.S. Army Corps of Engineers asked Cal-Am to postpone pursuit of a supersized dam so it could come up with its own plan for an even bigger dam. Fair game for all, the Carmel River was at the mercy of both private and government agencies. It took the Corps of Engineers nine years to draft its plan, and when it was unveiled, it was definitely bigger than Cal-Am's forty-thousand-acre-foot dream dam. The Corps of Engineers' big knockout punch at the Carmel River was a proposed 118,000-acre-foot "multipurpose" dam, nearly three times the size of Cal-Am's plan. It remains on a drawing board somewhere. There is a memento from the innovative fight the men and women of Cachagua waged against Cal-Am more than thirty years ago. It is a yellowing, old poster leaning against the wall of an upper shelf at the Cachagua General Store. It is straightforward in its message, unpretentious in its plea. It simply says, "Help."

Overlapping the pro-dam sentiment of the 1959 California Water Plan, was a gradual environmental consciousness occurring both nationally and statewide. Some of the early examples were in 1961, when California Tomorrow, a think tank for planning and conservation, was originally formed in the San Francisco Bay Area, and in 1965, when the Republican-led Planning and Conservation League was formed. At about the same period, the California Roadside Council, a Republican-supported anti-billboard group that tried to save Lake Tahoe, came into existence. In 1968 Congress passed the National Wild and Scenic Rivers System, and in 1969 Congress enacted the National Environmental Policy Act (NEPA), requiring that an environmental impact statement (EIS) be prepared before federal agencies took actions with potentially adverse environmental results.

Finally, in 1972, came the passage of the California Wild and Scenic Rivers Act. But as early as 1962, *California Going, Going . . .*, a publication of California Tomorrow, declared:

Our growing population is not only polluting California's air and water and making heavy demands upon its land. It is also swallowing in huge gulps that land's water. Shortages of water are not limited to the San Joaquin Valley and Metropolitan Los Angeles. Domestic, industrial, and agricultural shortages exist from Eureka to San Diego; and we are permitting our industries and farmers to develop by allowing them to take too much water out of underground basins. This is a weak foundation upon which to base the future welfare of a great state.

One of the pivotal issues to influence the future protection of California rivers, at least those in the northern region of the state, occurred from 1969 through 1972. In an oblique nod to the environment, California Governor Ronald Reagan killed the proposed Dos Rios Dam project on the Eel River in Mendocino County by withdrawing state support for the Corps of Engineers' project. Rancher Richard Wilson, a far-thinking Republican who later became a California Coastal commissioner and member of the California Forestry Commission, led the opposition to the dam, arguing that it would flood agricultural and Indian ancestral lands of Round Valley—but most significant to his cause was his reasoning that the dam was not economically viable.

Wilson considered himself a conservative, but at that time the description also meant a conservationist. The political infighting did not pit Republicans against Democrats or conservatives versus liberals. Instead, there was a strong bipartisan force that included members of both the state assembly and senate, who with their supporters took on the powerful Southern California water interests. While Reagan, who owned a ranch in Southern California, was not moved solely by potential environmental issues regarding the dam's impact on the river, he was convinced by the Wilson-led opposition that the Corps of Engineers offered no alternatives to the dam. It added to his political persona that he was also sympathetic to the Indians' complaints, which were cultural as well as environmental.

The U.S. Army Corps of Engineers had proposed a 730-foot-high dam that would have submerged Round Valley, along with four hundred archeological sites of the Yuki Tribe, under three hundred feet of water. The Corps' intention, agreed to by the California Department of Water Resources and its director, William Gianelli, was to supply water to Southern California and provide flood control and an artificial recreational lake of forty thousand surface acres. To stop a dam at the time was a signal that the ten-year-old California Water Plan was losing its clout, that water projects such as dams, flood controls, water storage, hydropower, and water supply to farms and cities could have a detrimental impact on the environment. This fledgling environmental stance was enforced in 1970, when California passed the California Environmental Quality Act (CEQA), requiring a similar review of projects as the federal government mandated. In 1972 State Senator Peter Behr, a liberal Republican and avowed conservationist from Marin County, pushed through his bill establishing the California Wild and Scenic Rivers Act. With the passage of this act, many rivers in the northwest region of California—including segments of the Eel River along with the Smith River and its tributaries, the Klamath River and its tributaries, and the Scott, Salmon, Trinity, Van Duzen, and American Rivers—all came under the state's protection.

But the type of environmental and conservation activism advocated by Peter Behr, Richard Wilson, California Tomorrow, and others was slow in arriving on the Monterey Peninsula. One of the earliest expressions of worry for the environmental health of the Carmel River did not arrive until 1974, when Ed Lee, a Carmel Valley resident, appeared at a California Public Utilities Commission (CPUC) meeting to oppose a Cal-Am rate hike for Carmel River water consumers. At the time, he argued that any further lowering of the river's water table, as suggested by the state's Department of Water Resources in its report supporting increasing the draw from the river's aquifers, would have "serious environmental consequences." Lee's concerns were for the river's riparian vegetation. Unrestricted pumping of the river's aquifer, as touted by the Department of Water Resources and carried out by Cal-Am, would have a serious impact on the river. Overpumping, coupled with a drought, would result in riparian mortality, which, in turn, would lead to stream-bank erosion. The CPUC did not address his warning. Lee's prediction of a riparian die-off came true during the 1976–77 drought, as Cal-Am's pumping of the river's aquifer went unchecked. Members of the Carmel Valley Property Owners Association, angered over the loss of river habitat, mounted a petition drive that eventually led to the formation of the Monterey Peninsula Water Management District (MPWMD) in 1978.

As concerns began to be expressed for the future of California's north coast rivers, the Carmel River, located not in the northwest region of the state but on the central coast, was turning into a dumping ground, and incongruously, Carmel Bay was declared an ecological reserve in 1975. Perhaps this is not surprising considering that the Monterey Peninsula's biggest concern about the river in the 1960s and '70s was its ability to meet the demands of population growth, not the river's environmental health. The Monterey Peninsula's social, political, and environmental mood for the Carmel River was drastically behind pace, not only with the changing times but with the rate the river was deteriorating. Once a refuge, the river was becoming a waste disposal site, as if whatever thrown there would be sucked down into infinity by the slow-moving current and disappear, forever out of sight and mind. Everything from winery discharge to waste materials from roadways dumped into feeder creeks to contamination from old, leaking septic systems, found its way into the river.

The Carmel River was not just a depository for faceless industrial waste, it was also misused by the very people who relied on it for their water. There was, for example, a young woman who was engaged to be married, but before the wedding her boyfriend broke the engagement. The young woman was furious, hurt, and bewildered. She went to stay with her brother who lived near the river, where she ranted and raved over the indignity and humiliation of being rejected. She threatened suicide, but instead she threw her diamond engagement ring into the Carmel River. Another time, a rowdy river boy trapped feral cats, threw them in the river, and then shot them with his .22 as they floated by. One winter, during flood-stage heavy rains, two men hauled an old refrigerator out of a café in Carmel Valley Village, trucked it to the river, and pushed it in. Out of sight, out of mind, the trashing of the Carmel River was well underway.

In the 1940s there was only one dredging operation removing rock, gravel, and sand from the river's bed. By the mid-1960s—as the environmental movement began to emerge—there were six dredging operations, each one steadily keeping pace with growth, and all six operating relatively free of environmental controls. In the decades of the 1960s and '70s, the river began to change as more subdivisions and golf courses were built along its banks. Ultimately, to protect expensive housing and recreational development, levees were built to contain the river during the winter rain months and direct it away from riverfront homes.

The Carmel River was losing its freedom to roam the valley floor and reacted by eroding its own banks when the winter rains came. To shore up the crumbling banks, old abandoned cars were cabled together and chain-linked like a lifeline from one washed-out slope to another. As if one band-aid remedy wasn't enough, old tires by the thousands were banded together and tossed into the river. By 1978 the degradation of the Carmel River was well underway, but still, water consumers and most politicians were more anxious about their supply of water from the river than they were about the river's health. That year, on June 6, voters, with the urging of the Carmel Valley Property Owners Association, formed the Monterey Peninsula Water Management District, giving the new agency a mandate to resolve their water problems.

Even with the endorsement of Congressman Leon Panetta, a Monterey native son, and the initial chairmanship of William Gianelli, former director of the California Department of Water Resources and a resident of the gated Pebble Beach community, the process of resolving the peninsula's water problems carried little public clout until 1993. The initial ineffectiveness of the MPWMD was explained this way: "By the early 1980s the policy makers, for reasons that had more to do with politics than with common sense, began to focus more and more intently on the idea of building a new and bigger dam on the Carmel River. . . . After thirty years and millions of dollars of studies, no one has been able to design a dam that is environmentally and financially justifiable," writes Keith Vandevere in "Water Over the Dam," a widely read and pirated unpublished study released by its author in 1998.

The new water management district was also handicapped by the recently passed Proposition 13, which included in its provisions that agencies with no history of taxation (such as the newly formed MPWMD) were not entitled to any share of county property tax revenues. The Monterey County Board of Supervisors gave the district only twenty-five thousand dollars of its revenue from taxes, which meant the directors of the new district had to seek state legislation to force the county to release additional operating cash to them. Later that year, 1978, Governor Jerry Brown signed legislation that transferred $180,000 of property tax revenues from Monterey County to the new district. Two years after taking the chair, in May 1980, Gianelli, an outspoken anticonservationist, resigned, stating he was frustrated with the district board's slow pace in solving the Monterey Peninsula's water problems. The next year President Reagan appointed Gianelli assistant secretary of the army for civil works, giving him authority over the civil works program of the U.S. Army Corps of Engineers. He resigned that position in 1984 to go into private consulting, but remained a resident of the Monterey Peninsula.

In late 1980, in response to a seriously eroding river and the ineffectiveness of efforts to prevent or control the erosion, Carmel Valley attorney Zan Henson filed a $2.8-million lawsuit against Cal-Am on behalf of nearly a dozen riverfront property owners. Henson sought compensation for erosion that occurred after riparian vegetation was killed by alleged overpumping. Henson was supported in his suit by geologist Robert Curry, of the University of California at Santa Cruz, who had been contracted to a three-year study of the river by the Monterey Peninsula Water Management District.

While Henson was awaiting a court date, the Monterey County Board of Supervisors, in 1981, banned all future development within two hundred feet of the Carmel River in a move to eliminate any new possibilities of property damage caused by an unruly river. But that action did nothing for existing property owners already living within the two-hundred-foot limit. Then, in early January 1982, about two hundred feet of riverbank washed away in one day of rain, and riverfront property owners in the Schulte Road area were in a panic. They petitioned the Monterey County Board of Supervisors to protect them against further erosion. Three months later the voter-approved Monterey Peninsula Water Management District mailed a survey to four hundred Carmel Valley residents asking if they would be willing to help pay $150,000 a year for a channel-restoration project. The next month, the storm-swollen river tore away a concrete barrier on the south bank, leaving supporting cables and timbers at the Schulte Road Bridge dangling in the swift current. Officials for the MPWMD said that if enough people were willing to share the costs of erosion control they would put the proposal on the upcoming November ballot—the same ballot the water board hoped would include a proposal for a new dam on the river.

But the water management district was holding a political football with no one on the receiving end. By May 1982, the MPWMD's proposal for a $150,000 river management project was encountering public resistance because the board was proposing that Carmel Valley property owners pay 51 percent of the cost, with Cal-Am ratepayers picking up the rest. Fees would be highest for riverfront property owners. By June the board of the MPWMD was deluding itself into thinking it could put a dam proposal on the quickly approaching November ballot along with the river management project—even though the board still could not agree on how to finance the management project. Some thought only riverfront property owners should pay, some that everyone in the watershed should pay, others that the Cal-Am ratepayers should pick up the bulk of the cost.

At the end of June 1982, the water board faced the fact that it could not have a dam proposal ready for a vote by November, but it continued to consider putting the river management project before the voters at that time—although MPWMD board members still had not come to an agreement on how to finance the project. Members were leaning toward setting up a Carmel Valley–wide assessment district, and only residents within this district would vote on the project. However, the water board did not resolve its problems soon enough to get the issue on the November ballot. The board was quickly sinking into a state of complete dysfunction: Directors were trading charges of conflict of interest and were frequently storming out of meetings. Two directors were running against each other for county supervisor and extremely volatile issues—like the proposed annexation of Carmel Valley Ranch, a subdivision development and golf course bordering the river—were distracting everyone's attention. The public was so irritated that the MPWMD board sometimes had to listen to more than an hour of angry public testimony before it could even take up its agenda.

In May 1983, a Monterey County Superior Court jury disagreed with Henson and Curry's contention that the river's erosion was caused by a riparian vegetation die-off resulting from overpumping. The jury, voting eleven to one in favor of Cal-Am, agreed with the water company's attorneys who argued that the

As if the devastating decade of the 1980s—when two hundred feet of riverbank washed away in one day—wasn't enough, the 1995 flood year came along, washing out more riverbank and threatening to capsize this house, approximately one mile downstream from Schulte Road Bridge. Courtesy of the Monterey Peninsula Water Management District.

erosion occurred as a result of drought conditions and a "false point" in the river, which created a diversion.

That same spring of 1983, the U.S. Soil Conservation Service (SCS), which had previously funded riverbank restoration, gave up its efforts, admitted defeat, and retreated from the Carmel River. In a letter signed by the state conservationist, the SCS, stated: "Spot treatment of severe erosion problems on the Carmel River has proven to be ineffective." With the withdrawal of SCS support, erosion control fell to the riverfront property owners.

As the U.S Soil Conservation Service was coming to its conclusion that small, or limited-area, treatment of the river's erosion wasn't working, the Monterey Peninsula Water Management District returned with its oft-revised proposal to form a Carmel River Management Zone. This plan required the

Concrete rubble, shown in this 1982 photo, was used in an attempt to shore up the banks of the river in the Schulte Road area of Carmel Valley. Courtesy of the Monterey Peninsula Water Management District.

approval of a majority of riverfront property owners because it would assess them collectively an estimated $45,000 a year toward funding riverbank restoration. Another $105,000 annually would come from water consumers outside the management zone, who would pay a $2.40 water fee each year.

In promoting the passage of a Carmel River Management Zone, Bruce Buel, manager of the water district, declared, "The Carmel River is totally out of control. It's totally out of equilibrium and it will continue to eat on itself until someone is able to control it." Buel went on to explain, "Clearly, we will not be able to replace the fifteen miles of river and its banks with rip rap and we don't even want to do that. We just want to minimize the erosion and river's deterioration. We want to keep it as natural as possible. We hope to use the funds to actually design structural improvements on the river without going into a Los Angeles River situation." Buel, noting that the Carmel River had even gained notoriety in Steinbeck's *Cannery Row*, admitted that the river had "been degraded so much over

Tons of concrete and hundreds of old tires were dumped into the river in an effort to prevent bank erosion. This 1982 photo is looking downstream toward the Schulte Road Bridge at the river's south bank. Courtesy of the Monterey Peninsula Water Management District.

the last forty years to the point that Steinbeck would not even recognize it today."

What apparently escaped Buel's attention was the fact that the Los Angeles River and the Carmel River were already more alike than anyone was willing to admit. In fact, there are startling similarities between the two rivers. The Los Angeles River in its beginnings was a narrow, shallow stream, much like the Carmel River. They both turned into destructive torrents of water, washing away their banks and farmlands during winter storms, and taking their course wherever they pleased. Like the Carmel River in the eighteenth century, the Los Angeles River attracted Spanish explorers who gave it its name. And the Los Angeles River, like the Carmel River, became a source of water for mission development and agriculture. As the city of Los Angeles grew, the river was virtually the only source of water for a growing and demanding population, providing both drinking and irrigation water—just like the Carmel River.

Before: By June 23, 1987, a dry river—at mid–Carmel Valley—underwent a thorough grading that covered existing concrete rubble with soil, sand, and gravel and softened the banks of the river. Known as the Berwick Project, the remake of the river at this junction helped reduce the probability of erosion. The river was dry following a harsh drought period combined with pumping of the river's aquifer. Courtesy of the Monterey Peninsula Water Management District.

Even Los Angeles's legal right to the exclusive use of the Los Angeles River parallels the legal rights attached to the Carmel River. Gradually, water from the Los Angeles River was needed solely for domestic use, and as demand increased, the aquifers of the Los Angeles River were pumped to keep pace with that demand. Toward the end of the Los Angeles River—or the end of its *appearing* like a river—flood control projects by the U.S. Army Corps of Engineers turned it into a concrete bed that today resembles a highway more than a river bed. The similarities did not end with the rivers' beginnings and their demise. They both became laboratories for extensive studies by scientists, environmental organizations, and government agencies— all similarly coming to inconclusive findings. Ultimately the conservation organization American Rivers declared the Los Angeles River the most endangered waterway in the United

After: Evidence of the success of the Berwick Project can be seen fifteen years later in this photo taken on May 20, 2002, from the same location as the 1987 photo. Courtesy of the Monterey Peninsula Water Management District.

States. This was in 1995, just four years before the Carmel River would be anointed with the same dubious distinction.

The ten-year Carmel River management project required an engineer to develop "a structural management plan" for the entire length of the river—not just the fifteen miles referred to by Buel. In promoting the concept of the Carmel River Management Zone, there was no mention of engaging any environmental expertise. Ballots went out to 758 registered voters who were residents of the proposed assessment zone. A total of 445 ballots were returned to the water management district and of those, 367 people voted to assess themselves in order to shore up the banks of the river. This was an impressive 82.5 percent in favor of not only a river management zone but of taxing themselves, as well. Via hindsight, there are river activists today who look back and see the 1983 landslide vote for a river management zone as the turning point when an awareness for the environmental well-being of the Carmel River began. Even so, in the winter of 1983 tons of concrete rubble were dumped in the river

Red and arroyo willows watered by drip lines were systematically planted to stabilize the erosion-prone north bank in the mid–Carmel Valley area. Photo dated September 1987. Courtesy of the Monterey Peninsula Water Management District.

in a riprap effort to stop the erosion of its banks. The concrete came from a variety of places, including the San Carlos Hotel in downtown Monterey, which was being demolished to make room for a new, more modern hotel. Salvaged concrete also came from Cannery Row buildings being torn down in the wake of the sardines' disappearance, and from a school in nearby Seaside. The river's death knell was concrete. The timing couldn't have been more devastating for a stream being transformed from a naturally flowing body of water into a captured river manipulated, engineered, and channelized.

It would be 1984 before an actual river management plan would be set in place, and then it only covered the lower fifteen miles of the river for a ten-year period. The intent of the management plan was not to return the river to its natural form, but rather to eliminate—or at least try to control—erosion caused by high runs or flooding, principally by rebuilding riverbanks and planting vegetation. Included in the plan was the goal of returning the steelhead to the river. But even with a well-intentioned management plan in place, by the end of the 1980s the Carmel River, where it passed through rapidly developing Carmel Valley, was lined with concrete. And the onslaught continued. In about 1987 the U.S. Army Corps of Engineers also deposited concrete rubble along the riverbanks, but it washed away. And following the 1989 Loma Prieta Earthquake, a bridge on Highway 1 had to be removed and rebuilt. The concrete from that bridge also went into the river.

Slowly, but inevitably, the river was becoming more and more like the Los Angeles River, in spite of Buel's earlier concerns. While the Los Angeles River was engineered into an urban, concrete-lined drainage system for an asphalt-covered watershed, the rural Carmel River was slowly being lined with concrete rubble softened only by riparian vegetation planted by the property owners acting not only in good faith but in their own economic interests. The frontier boundary of the river, naturally dividing creeping urbanization on the north side from wilderness on the south, was beginning to blur. In less than the span of two decades, the river was no longer its original self. And in less than a half century, the river had moved from purity to pollution. And it all came to rest in the lagoon.

Its lagoon is the final indicator of the river's health. In the summer, when its water is shallow, it acts like a solar collector with freshwater on top of salt water. It is critical to the steelhead juveniles who are dependent on streamflows to sustain quality habitat, not only in the mainstem but also in the lagoon throughout the summer and fall months—a period when the river goes completely dry because of overdrafts of the wells and aquifers. Without a normal flow to the ocean, it can become stagnant and polluted. As early as 1947, there was a government explanation that "stagnation, augmented by hot weather and effluent from the nearby sewage treatment plant" appears to be the cause of the death of thousands of steelhead fingerlings in the lagoon at the mouth of the Carmel River. Who was paying attention? As recently as 1985 no one was taking any interest in or responsibility for coastal lagoons like the Carmel River's because no one saw any value in lagoons.

In August 1988, the Monterey County Environmental Health Department posted warnings at three locations on the river. There were dangerous amounts of fecal coliform in the water. One of the locations was the lagoon, where the level of fecal coliform was nearly four times the safety standard set by California regulations. The cause of the fecal coliform was unknown—whether from humans or animals—but officials speculated that it had accumulated to such high levels because parts of the river were stagnant. It was the second year in a row that the Carmel River didn't have enough water to flow to the ocean. The river's obituary was being written in the sand.

Voters had formed the Monterey Peninsula Water Management District in 1978 with a mandate to resolve their water problems, but efforts at restoration of the river's banks, as an example, had more to do with property values than it did with restoring the river. In answer to the problems inherent to the river's erosion patterns, voters approved the Carmel River Management Zone in 1983, and it was 1984 before a meager river management plan was adopted. Then, in 1993, still concerned with the question of supply rather than the environmental condition of the river, a measure to fund a desalination plant was defeated. The public wasn't sure which way to turn, but it wasn't willing to accept an increase in water rates in order to finance an expensive water-conversion plant that would take the pressure off the river.

Then, two years later, in 1995, voters voiced their opinion once again and in doing so began steadily to embrace environmental sensitivities for the river. This time they voted against building any dam on the Carmel River. A dam, the voting majority decided, was not the answer to their water supply or to the eventual restoration of the river. It was far too expensive and it would encourage more growth and thereby allow additional connections to the peninsula-wide water system, leaving individual households with less water in a drought because there would be more users and no actual increase in water supply. Furthermore, it had the potential of delivering the death blow to the steelhead migrating upstream after a hiatus in the ocean. With this concern for the steelhead, environmental awareness was beginning to take hold. The public came to these conclusions despite not having been given all the information available to them by a local newspaper. "Shortly before the 1995 election, a reporter for a local paper explained privately that he had refrained from reporting the facts which reflected badly on the dam because he felt that the water district staff had worked so hard for so long that it would be unfair not to let them build the dam," Vandevere wrote in a footnote to his 1998 "Water Over the Dam" study.   But now the public had backed itself into a corner. It didn't want a desalination plant nor did it want another dam on the river. While the citizens of the Monterey Peninsula basked in what they thought was an anti-dam victory, Cal-Am came back in 1997 and snubbed the public's majority vote, saying that in spite of public sentiment against a dam they would build one anyway; they didn't need consumer approval—just like in 1921 and 1949 when the San Clemente and Los Padres Dams were built. Then, in 1999, for the first time since the formation of the Monterey Peninsula Water Management District, voters elected an anti-dam majority to its board. Now the line was clearly drawn between the desires of the water consumers and those of Cal-Am, the water provider. With an anti-dam majority on the board of the very agency created to resolve water resource problems for the Monterey Peninsula, the political swing was in sync with public opinion, but the Carmel River no longer resembled the free-flowing little stream that had attracted Spanish explorers and capitalistic entrepreneurs centuries before.

In March 1999, American Rivers, a national advocacy group dedicated to the protection and restoration of North American rivers, listed the Carmel River as one of the continent's ten most endangered rivers. The listing was based upon threats to the river that included "overpumping, nonpoint source pollution, continued development in the floodplain, the proposed development of a new dam on the river, and the need for greater public awareness of issues affecting the river." With that grim assessment, the relatively miniscule Carmel River joined the ranks of such previously listed rivers as the American, Los Angeles, Kings, Merced, and Kern in California, and on a national scale the Klamath, Columbia, Snake, Mississippi, Rio Grande, and the Everglades.

Whether a repository for concrete rubble or a diamond engagement ring, it was obvious that when it came to trashing the Carmel River nothing was too good for it, or too bad. Monterey, the community that historically depended on the river for its water source, was among the contributors to the river's gradual demise.

In retrospect, dating back to the building of the Hotel Del Monte in 1880, domestic water from the Carmel River had always been in short supply. Once the hotel was built, more water was needed, so the Chinese Dam was placed on the river. Once the year-round populations of Pacific Grove and Monterey began to burgeon, yet more water was needed, so the San Clemente Dam was constructed. When more tourists arrived, again more water was needed. Once Carmel-by-the-Sea began to fill out, even more water was needed, and that put further strain on a limited supply, although the village's growth never matched the rest of the Monterey Peninsula. So there never was enough water coming from the Carmel River to meet the demand. The watershed and the river could provide only so much water. No matter how frequently dams were built to hold back the water draining into the Carmel River, they could never keep up with the increasing demand for water, an artificial or trumped-up demand imposed by development on a real and limited resource. Ultimately, that demand would have a devas-

The Carmel River's lagoon remains tranquil most of the year, but heavy winter runoff from the river's watershed annually carries the threat of flooding nearby expensive homes unless the mouth of the river is breached. Courtesy of the Monterey Peninsula Water Management District.

tating effect on the living body of the Carmel River and on the land the people called paradise.

By the mid- to late 1990s, after capturing water from the river for seventy-nine years, the reservoir behind the San Clemente Dam was nearly filled with sediment. Of the original 1,450 acre feet of water storage, only 150 acre feet remained. In 1992 the Division of Dam Safety of the California Department of Water Resources declared the dam unsafe. An earthquake of 6.5 magnitude or greater could cause a failure, or a heavy flood could "overtop" the dam and undermine its structures. Opponents of the dam started a campaign to remove the dam from the river. As the twentieth century was coming to a close, Los Padres Dam, completed at the end of 1948, had only 1,500 acre feet of storage remaining compared to its original 3,030 acre feet. Nothing had been decided as to the fate of the San Clem-

The first of two dramatic photos of a breached Carmel River lagoon was taken on June 22, 2006. Both images capture the power of the river as it empties into the ocean. Courtesy of the Monterey Peninsula Water Management District.

ente Dam. Meanwhile, the reservoir behind the Los Padres Dam was slowly filling with silt.

Gradually it was becoming apparent to the public that reservoirs behind dams were as good—perhaps even better—at trapping sediment as they were at storing water. But if the Carmel River was to be put on life support, it was the fish in the river— the steelhead—that held the key to the river's health. The river and the steelhead are one, without one there is not the other.

This second photograph of the breached Carmel River lagoon (note the presence of people on the banks) was taken on February 16, 2008, nearly two years after the first photograph. Courtesy of the Monterey Peninsula Water Management District.

9 〰 DEMISE OF THE STEELHEAD

Anglers Debate the Fate of the Fish

The placement of another dam on the Carmel River in 1949 posed a serious threat to the steelhead migrating from seawater to freshwater during their spawning periods. The status of this native game fish was more important to anglers in the mid-twentieth century than to anyone interested in the well-being of the river. But the steelhead were a visible barometer and easy indicator of the river's health. Protection of the fish was included in the design of the Los Padres Dam. To protect the steelhead a "rescue pool" would be installed on the downstream face of the dam. During the steelhead run each year, the fish would "climb" steps to the rescue pool to avoid possible floodwaters. The plan was then for the fish to be mechanically transported up the face of the dam to the storage upstream by means of a specially built fish elevator, which apparently was never constructed. In its absence, steelhead fingerlings were trucked in by the can-load, hoisted on mules, and packed upstream from the reservoir where volunteers said their silent prayers as the fish were transplanted into river ponds behind the reservoir.

How the fish got back downstream and eventually to the ocean was up to them. After growing up in the vast depths of the Pacific Ocean, steelhead confront a huge unsurpassable concrete wall of the Los Padres Dam's spillway after first instinctively finding their home waters at the mouth of the Carmel River. Then they must wind their way upriver through shallow pools and riffles, adjust to water temperature changes, and adapt their kidneys from ocean water to freshwater. Finally, they must find an engineer's solution to answer nature's spawning necessity: a small, square opening about three feet across with water pouring down it, possibly simulating a small tributary.

Today, there is a fish ladder that enters the pool in front of the Los Padres Dam at about a forty-five-degree angle on the west bank. Any fish determined to climb this "ladder" of aluminum, covered with a heavy-gauge wire mesh, will not reach the solitude of shallow eddies perfect for embedding its eggs in the dam's reservoir, but will instead land in a large, ten-foot, cinder-block holding tank, or walled-in cage, where it will cruise in circles until a truck pulls up and attaches an appendage to the connecting pipe to transport the fish to the reservoir. Locals call this method "trap and truck."

It could have been an idyllic scene if all there was to witness was the sun setting over the lagoon that early evening in February 1984. But for someone familiar with what was taking place in plain view, the glow of the evening at the mouth of the Carmel River was far from a romantic end-of-the-day interlude.

There, on the hard-packed beach between the incoming tide and the trickling ankle-high river, was a man in chest-high fishing waders down on his knees scooping out sand with his hands. Innocent enough to the casual witness, the man was frantically trying to open a passage between the river and the ocean to entice the homebound steelhead upstream. There was nothing altruistic about his efforts. He was a renegade fisherman hoping to snare the prized steelhead as it followed the scent of the river back to where it was born, to the spawning gravel at the Carmel's headwaters once again.

"Those fish are unique," said a man watching the scene. "They're not like other steelhead in other streams. They're stronger, bigger, and they fight harder."

The observer didn't say anything more. He didn't need to explain further. He was a believer, as everyone on the river who fished for the steelhead were believers. The Carmel River was reputed, whether myth or not, to contain the most wily, ornery, meaty, and difficult-to-land fish on the West Coast. A solidly hooked steelhead could cause an angler to panic and run after it just to keep a ten-pound test leader from snapping or the line from completely spooling out in a split second. Carmel River steelhead were big muscle fish, prized for their tenacity and fighting spirit. To catch and actually land one was a feat that you could wear as a trophy for all to see and envy. But envy wasn't the only emotion you might feel when you saw one landed and exhibited for all the world to see. There was also greed. Dedicated anglers, like the one in waders frantically trying to entice the steelhead up the river by hand-scooping a trough from ocean to river, would do anything to claim a steelhead for themselves.

That February there was an unusually high run of steelhead in the Carmel River, and the combination of low flows and clear water created a severe enforcement problem for the California Department of Fish and Game. Water flow that winter was between 100 and 150 cubic feet per second. The larger cobbles and boulders were exposed in the wide areas of the channel and a sturdy, sure-footed angler could easily cross it. The river was full, but it wasn't wild or threatening. Watching it make its way through the lower valley, it could be called a happy creek. Still, the fish pooled up.

The problem was that the big fish returning from the ocean to their home spawning grounds were so numerous and visible that outlaw anglers were using every illegal trick they knew to catch them. They stopped at nothing in their fever to take the steelhead. They tramped through willows and threw rocks to scare resting fish from their cover. They used pitchforks, gill nets, explosives, and various kinds of homebuilt snagging gear like chicken wire traps to capture the fish. The fish they didn't keep, they sold to local restaurants.

"The fish are easy targets for snaggers," complained Nate Swift, a local sports-shop owner at that time, "and there is a lot of snagging going on. It is readily apparent to anyone fishing the river. It is unbelievable what is going on. On top of that, there should be water in the river all year. We have fish dying because there is no water."

Pitchforking steelhead isn't new to the river, or most likely any other coastal stream in California with a history of native steelhead. Killing steelhead with pitchforks has been common as far south as Malibu Creek in Southern California. In his 1937 poem, "Steelhead," Robinson Jeffers tells the story of a gypsy girl using a "five-tined hay-fork" to spear steelhead in the Carmel River:

Hay-fork at her head's height; suddenly she darted it
     down like
a heron's beak and panting hard
Leaned on the shaft, looking down passionately, her
     gipsy-lean
face, then stooped and dipping
One arm to the little breasts she drew up her catch,
     great hammered-
silver steelhead with the tines through it

She is caught by a young rancher on horseback and must pay for her crime of trespassing and spearing the fish by retreating to an island of warm willows where she willingly has sex with him. Afterward the young rider laments a scene at the mouth of the river where herring gulls are attacking stranded steelhead and gouging out their eyes.

Unlike the gypsy girl, outlaw fishermen don't always rely on pitchforks. Their favorite method of taking a steelhead is by *gaunching* (pronounced locally as "gonching"). Poachers use a large albacore hook with a cord attached to it and a willow switch as a pole. They work in pairs, with one person on the bank and the other in the water using a facemask for spotting the hiding fish. The spotter's job is locate the fish and once it's gaunched, throw it on the bank. The only evidence they leave behind are fish scales, blood, and trampled brush.

A veteran game warden gave this description of gaunching steelhead on the Carmel River.

As water levels drop and clarity improves, poachers scout the known holes where steelhead rest on their upstream spawning migration. This includes undercut banks, particularly where large trees hang out over the water. The branches of these trees offer a perch for the poachers, who lay on the lowest branch to the water and look into the hole or undercut bank with a face mask or other underwater viewing device, which are illegal gear along the central coast rivers and streams. This device could be a coffee can with Plexiglas glued to one open end, or something similar, but face masks have been the usual tool.

When a large steelhead is spotted below the poacher, either he or his lookout, will break off a local willow branch about four to five feet long. The branch isn't of a large diameter, just strong enough to wrap nylon parachute-type cord around the hook shank at the end of the branch, and firm enough to be lowered straight down into the water without bending against any current.

With the hook shank bound to the willow by the cord, and the remaining length of cord spiraled up the branch to the person's hand, the branch is lowered next to a fish and the large-gap hook is quickly yanked upwards into the belly of the fish. At this point, the set-up would look like a homemade gaff of sorts.

Once the fish is impaled, the weight of the fish and the quick upward motion unwraps the cord from the willow branch, allowing it to fall into the water and drift out of sight. Hard to find evidence for a warden. The violator lifts the fish, cord, and hook, hand-over-hand out of the water and onto the bank, where it is usually killed by a blow to the head with a rock or branch. At this point the person taking the fish either grabs it and runs, or their assistant takes it and hides it under brush and leaves, depending upon the time of day and human activity on the river.

Because these poachers aren't always found walking with one another, they may split up and meet somewhere else, only to return after dark to retrieve the steelhead from the brush. The wet cord and hook are often wrapped into a small, flat bundle and stuffed into something like a chewing tobacco tin, which is carried in a pocket. The face mask may be stuffed inside a loose-fitting jacket or shirt as the poacher tries to "blend in" with others in the area or walks onto a nearby road to be picked up by the lookout, who had departed earlier.

Pretty slick operation that I've had the good fortune to watch while hiding in the bushes nearby a few times in my career. If the warden yells "Stop, police!" or "Stop, game warden!" a footrace usually ensues. This type of patrol takes a lot of dedicated time and is best done with wardens paired with a partner.

To my knowledge, this type of illegal activity was "discovered" on our local waters and isn't seen much outside the central coast, except where our "locals" travel to other steelhead waters to practice their illegal activities.

That February 1984, the California Department of Fish and Game called in eight wardens to work the river on weekends, and thirty-five citations were written in one three-week period. In one case, two poachers snagged one fish and were arguing over whose fish it was when the warden stepped up and nabbed them.

Outlaw fishermen were not the only ones putting pressure on the steelhead in February 1984. A dozen or more men with legal fishing licenses in their chest waders could be seen at locally known "hot spots" standing in water that barely wet their ankles. Elbow to elbow, shoulder to shoulder, they flip cast underhanded in a style that evolved from not enough room for man, fish, or river. They used oakie drifters with bright orange yarn attached to a short-shank hook for shallow water, or they tried spin and glows, little cleos, corkies, and hot shots, whatever might attract the eye of a hungry steelhead. And they frequently used a buddy system, where one angler would let the steelhead take his line out of sight and another would assist in landing the hard-fighting steelhead, a practice far from ethical if not illegal.

Even the leaders of the local fishing groups saw how ludicrous the situation had become. Basing their arguments on water flow, they wanted stiffer regulations on when fishing would be allowed. But they were divided on how much water flow was needed before the river would be open to fishing. The Carmel River Steelhead Association wanted to see a law mandating two hundred cubic feet per second, arguing that it would cut down on illegal fishing. Monterey County Unified Sportsmen's Association argued that such a proposal wouldn't stop illegal fishing and was actually a smokescreen to eventually close the river to all fishing. The Steelhead Association argued, "If they're legal fishermen, they'll go for the two hundred cubic feet per second." There were suspicions among the Unified Sportsmen that the other group actually wanted to close the Carmel to all fishing. A Steelhead spokesman, when pressed, said he ultimately would like to see a catch-and-release law at 150 cubic feet per second, but he was doubtful the State Fish and Game Commission would go for it.

Nate Swift, the sports-shop owner, stood squarely between the two groups.

"If we can get people to realize what sad shape that river is in, then we've done a world of good," he said.

Mas Yokogawa was president of the Steelhead Association in 1984 and also in the middle of the controversy. His approach to the debate was on the side of conservation.

"Basically the river is dry from the bridge down," Yokogawa said. "That's why we rescue fish every year. Otherwise there won't be fish in the Carmel River. In the 1950s there was a definite channel in the river and fish were in deeper water. The fish weren't in one area, they were scattered throughout the river. The fish are critical. We're one of the last streams down the coast with steelhead. I hate to see the fish being taken when there is no water. It's a conservation effort. We need to conserve more water in the winter. When there is more water they can't see the fish and snag them. Some people just have to take that fish when they see it—legally or illegally."

"This macho stuff, snagging fish," he continues. "The father snags and passes it down to the son. It's a way of life for a lot of people. It's not a sport right now, it's meat fishing. We don't want to regulate the river, but we don't want to see it go downhill. We're trying to conserve what we got. There's not too much pressure, there's too much snagging. If everyone fished legal there would be no problem. We just have to get more water. With more hotels and growth we're going to have less water. The way we see it, we're trying to save the fish we have now. In the long run we have to save the fish."

Just how endangered were the steelhead of the Carmel River in 1984? The Steelhead Association said the historical run was two thousand fish. The Unified Sportsmen said that was low, and the regional patrol captain for Fish and Game said his agency didn't have an official count. So no one knew precisely what the fishing impact—whether legal or illegal—was to the steelhead. Meanwhile, there weren't enough game wardens to police the river full time.

Would another dam on the Carmel River solve the fishing debate, if, as proponents say, it could guarantee water in the river year-round?

Nate Swift answered.

"Unfortunately, we've gone past the point where we need it. What we need to do is make sure the same thing doesn't happen twenty years from now."

Downstream from Robles del Rio, at a bedrock outcrop of the Tularcitos Formation, is Chalk Rock pool. On February 26, 1984, I fished alone on the Chalk Rock curve. There had been no sign of steelhead in this pool, so when I felt a lugging tug on the line I thought I had snagged a submerged tree. I started upstream to release the snag but the tug moved slowly with me. It couldn't be a steelhead because there was no thrashing and brutal run. It was probably the current and a water-soaked log teasing my line. To be safe, I started to reel in, not putting too much pressure on the line just in case I had unknowingly hooked an infamous Carmel River steelhead. The line went out. I reeled in. The line moved slowly but forcefully out. "Fish on!" as my fishing friends yell in order to release just enough adrenalin to remain calm. I have no idea how long I played the fish, or how long it played me. My intent was to land it. When I did, I stooped to take in its silvery length and girth and only then did I realize I had drawn a crowd of fishing spectators. "Nice fish," someone said. "Going to keep it?" No, I wasn't. It looked too spent to me, and as much as I like a steelhead steak, I released it back into the pool where it glided into its depth. The spectators drifted away, disinterested in trying for a fish I had just released. Excited to share my story, I drove to Carmel Valley Village where I knew friends were having lunch at a cafe. And there they were, sitting in their chest waders, eating hamburgers. When I told them my story, they didn't say a word other than to ask again where I had caught the steely, and then two of them just got up and went back to the Chalk Rock curve and caught that fish again. This time they kept it. They took pictures of each other grinning and holding that thirteen-pound steelhead. And then they took it home. It was one of the last steelhead ever caught on the Carmel River. And they knew it.

Within two years, in 1986, a new Fish and Game regulation automatically closed the Carmel River to steelhead fishing from November 16 to February 28 when the flow was below two hundred cubic feet per second. An accompanying "sweetener" regulation opened the stream to daily fishing instead of the usual three-day-a-week routine when the flow exceeded two hundred cubic feet per second. The California Department of Fish and

Game was committed to a three-year trial of the two-hundred-cubic-feet-per-second regulation, but no one knew for certain if it was a realistic measure for protecting the fish.

"We don't know if the two hundred cubic feet per second is the answer," admitted a regional patrol captain at the time, "but we're committed to it for three years. If it's not a good tool, we should change it."

As it turned out, the two-hundred-cubic-feet-per-second rule solved no one's argument as to when the river should be open and when it should be closed. Adding to the problem was a three-year drought, from 1988 to 1990, when the river never breached its sandbar at the mouth, making it tragically inaccessible to steelhead coming home to spawn. Before the decade of the '90s would end, the cubic-feet-per-second (cfs) restriction in the regulations would drop to 150 cfs and then to 135 cfs, meaning that the river was closed to all fishing when its flow did not reach those modest numbers. The original, and more restrictive, 200-cfs criteria did not work. Meanwhile the numbers of steelhead returning to the Carmel River continued to decline while the river remained open to fishing. By 1991 only one adult steelhead was seen at the San Clemente Dam fish ladder. The next year there were only fourteen adult steelhead in the river. The California Department of Fish and Game, blaming the three-year drought and "potential angling impact to a severely depressed population" for the decline in fish, closed the river. It would stay closed until 1998.

The California Department of Fish and Game's decision to close the Carmel River wasn't any more scientific than the anglers' belief that the fish could be protected based on the cubic-feet-per-second rule. It took another two years, in 1993, before the steelhead numbers in the river reached a miniscule but hopeful comeback, estimated at 285 fish.

Optimism for the return of the steelhead was an emotional roller coaster. In 1994 the official steelhead numbers reached an alarming low when a fish count at San Clemente Dam revealed that only ninety steelhead passed through the fish-way. In 1995 the run was up to 590 adults as the effects of the drought began to subside. However, the steelhead numbers weren't that encouraging to the National Marine Fisheries Service, and in 1996, citing a "precipitous decline in steelhead populations," it proposed that the fish be listed as threatened or endangered under the federal Endangered Species Act (ESA). Fishermen were learning that the steelhead was not just a game fish, there for the thrill of catching one. Like humans who rely on clean water as part of their environment, steelhead also need clean, healthy streams, rivers, and lagoons to survive and multiply. The two—humans and fish—have a mutual dependence on a common resource. Still, solid scientific data were meager when it came to the specific steelhead of the Carmel River. That same year, 1996, a study by the California Department of Fish and Game admitted that "of all of California's steelhead stocks, the southern stocks (including the Carmel River) are the least known. This is mainly due to the scarcity and near-extirpation of the fish. Because there is no significant sport fishery for steelhead, there has been little impetus for research and assessment." In other words, when the numbers of steelhead dropped out of sight, license-buying or revenue-producing sports groups finally got worried and the department started to take the plight of the steelhead seriously.

The California Department of Fish and Game didn't stop at placing more stringent regulations on the river below the dams in 1996. There was a theory that the summer fishing season was having a negative impact on the juvenile and smolt steelhead that were naturally produced in the river above the dams. So a new regulation was added mandating the sole use of artificial lures with barbless hooks. The take was limited to five trout, of which only two could be rainbow trout ten inches or greater in total length. The upstream boundary for steelhead fishing is Rosie's Bridge, meaning that no steelhead can be taken above that point.

In 1997, on August 18, it was the federal government (not the state) that finally listed the central California coast steelhead, including the Carmel River run, as a threatened species under the Endangered Species Act (ESA). But the demise of the steelhead continued. In 1997 Dave Dettman, senior fisheries biologist for the Monterey Peninsula Water Management District (MPWMD), counted 289 dead juvenile steelhead in the Robinson Canyon to Shulte Road reach of the Carmel River. The agency's newsletter reported: "Dettman observed that the cause of the fish kill was due to no, or minimal, flows and high water temperatures. The fish kill was attributed to pumping rates at Cal-Am wells in excess of stream flows and recharge capacity. If these allegations are true, Cal-Am's practices could be significantly affecting a fish species that National Marine Fisheries Service has listed for protection under the ESA." In 1998 the California Department of Fish and Game reopened the river to wild steelhead fishing on a catch-and-release basis only, rationalizing that opening the river would "provide more opportunities for anglers and came as a result of a public recommendation." There was no mention by the department of any cubic-feet-per-second criteria. In effect, the anglers didn't have to wait twenty years, or until 2004, to see what would happen, as Nate Swift surmised in 1984. Ironically, it took less than two decades of unrealistic but stringent regulations based on water flow, combined with a dramatic decline in returning steelhead numbers, before the fishermen voluntarily submitted themselves to regulations that had no supporting data behind them.

None of their arguments for state-imposed fishing regulations relying on cubic feet per second were ever based on scientific fact. Both groups of anglers on the Carmel River were speculating. "Their arguments were based solely on personal experience acquired while fishing the river," explained Kevan Urquhart, Dettman's successor as senior fisheries biologist for the MPWMD, years later. "They were restricting themselves to no benefit." In Urquhart's view, the debate was eventually reduced to basic science: it was all about water in the river and the quality of habitat for the fish.

"It was not a matter of how many fish were lost to poachers, or how much pressure the fish were getting from anglers," explained Urquhart, stressing that his opinions do not necessarily reflect the position of the MPWMD. "They settled on two hundred cubic feet per second," Urquhart said, "but the anglers soon realized that there was no fishing because the river's not at 200 cubic feet per second that often. It's either under or it's way over. So they negotiated down to 150 cubic feet per second and even at that, most years there were less than ten days fishing the whole season."

Gradually, other restrictions were added to the cubic-feet-per-second condition, such as artificial lures with barbless hooks and catch-and-release. Furthermore, restricting fishing to three days a week effectively closed the river more than half the time, even when the minimum flows were met.

"The river became the most restricted river for fishing anywhere in the state at the time," Urquhart said. "It was like bird watching; you're not going to bring the steelhead back by no fishing. They left the river and never came back. It was a heartfelt effort by the anglers, but there is no evidence that it did any good because it did not stop the decline."

To put this in historical perspective, the Carmel River steelhead run has been estimated at twelve thousand to twenty thousand adult fish prior to 1850, making it the second largest steelhead fishery south of San Francisco. Probably the largest steelhead fishery is the Santa Ynez River near Santa Barbara, where historical runs reached an estimated twenty-five thousand steelhead. Adult returns to the Carmel River at the end of the twentieth century were estimated in the hundreds, or at approximately a 90 percent decline. By mid-twentieth century—1964 to 1975—the average annual run was an estimated 3,177 steelhead, or about 25 percent of historic levels. At one time the Carmel River supported over ten thousand angling hours per year, but by the 1990s the few fishermen on the river could be counted by the tens at most, and angling hours could be measured by a few days each season. The largest fishery today south of San Francisco is the San Lorenzo River, whose headwaters originate in the Santa Cruz Mountains. The Big Sur River is second and the Carmel River a distant third, according to Urquhart.

"The Carmel River angler has been restricted to death, but the run has hardly rebounded," observed Urquhart. "It is hypothetical whether low-flow closures will have any benefit. People make the mistake of trying to discourage poachers. They simply run anglers off the river so they can no longer report on the poachers. Well-meaning anglers, under the hope the fisheries would come back, were responsible for the regulations."

Was it too late to save the river and the steelhead?

Actually, the river and the steelhead were one and the same. There could not be a river such as the Carmel River, with its history of the legendary steelhead, without the fish, and conversely there could not be the mighty steelhead without the river. The Carmel River might survive without the fish but it would not be the same river. Steelhead numbers had dropped to an incredible low of one fish at the San Clemente fish-way in 1991. Demonstrating an amazing will to live and return to their home spawning grounds, there were fourteen the next year and ninety by 1994. But by 1997—as the twentieth century was seeing its last days—sadly, so was the steelhead. Designating the steelhead as "threatened" was comforting, but "threatened" was an understatement that left the lingering question, How could a fish that had once entered the Carmel River by the thousands be merely a "threatened" species when only a few dozen were now making their way back to their original spawning grounds? And what was going to be done about such a humiliating catastrophe as the loss of this great fish? The river had gone from purity to pollution, and the steelhead was its prime victim.

The alarm had been sounded, not once but many times, and finally it was being heard. The California Department of Fish and Game joined the Carmel River Steelhead Association and the Monterey Bay Salmon and Trout Project in a joint and desperate effort to restore the fish to its home river. Together, they started a "captive broodstock project" for rearing and releasing over 180,000 juvenile steelhead into the river's watershed. By the fall of 1996, fish counts had increased to an estimated three hundred fish and there was optimism that while the numbers were well below historic levels, nonetheless the steelhead was gradually recovering from near extinction.

A 1996 newsletter from the California Department of Fish and Game stated:

> It remains the Department's intent to eventually reopen the Carmel River steelhead fishing season, but only when a reliable self-sustaining steelhead population becomes evident. If the adult steelhead returns to the San Clemente Dam continue to show signs of recovery over the next two years, the Department will begin discussions to possibly reopen the Carmel River to winter steelhead fishing. Although the Department has established a goal of more than 1,000 adult steelhead arriving in two consecutive years before entertaining proposals for the harvest of fish, the Department is considering criteria for the reopening of the river to a catch-and-release, zero-bag-limit fishery prior to reaching that goal. The Department will continue its efforts to restore this steelhead resource and sport fishery.

The steelhead was still listed as a threatened species in 1998 when the California Department of Fish and Game reopened the river to fishing. If steelhead in healthy numbers are a significant barometer for a healthy river, both the Carmel River and its fish were in a sorry state by the end of the twentieth century. Saving the steelhead meant saving the river, but saving the river required a unified water management plan and the support of a dedicated public interest. And against a background of fish-count statistics and the politics of seeking another dam was the lingering threat of fire in the watershed. Twenty-two years after the devastating Marble-Cone Fire, there had not been any "pre-scribed" or controlled burns in the Los Padres National Forest in all those years, and the watershed was prime tinder.

The only insult left, after humans had abused and denigrat-ed the river, was for nature to add its final scorn, the burning of all the Carmel River drainage in Los Padres National Forest. A major fire could irreparably damage the river's watershed and turn the river into an inorganic string of slime-contam-inated drinking water held back by the already clogged res-ervoirs. A long, slow-burning fire would track itself down the subterranean paths of tree and brush roots, smoldering for days and weeks before opening old wounds in the sides of the can-yons, and from them would flow a long winter of milky brown self-destructive sludge. But, of course, this is the view from the banks of the Carmel River, not nature's more magnanimous view. A good fire from nature's vantage might be what the river needed most—a thorough flushing.

Fires in the forest are the biggest enemy of the river and the people living downstream who are dependent on the river for their domestic water. That's one reason the U.S. Forest Service, the pet creation of President Teddy Roosevelt, was established in 1905, partially to prevent fires and to protect the watershed. Fires in the watershed not only burned buildings put up by set-tlers, but more significantly, fires were destroying the protec-tive cover of the land itself. When vegetation binding the soil in place on the steep hillsides was burned off, the lowlands were flooded with tons of silt washing down. In 1869 uncontrolled fires were reported to be burning the California coastal range from Monterey to San Diego. Uncontrolled fires, particularly in the watershed feeding the Carmel River, would continue to be a serious threat and perplexing issue.

10 〰️ THE FINAL INSULT

Fire in the Forest

On September 8, 1999, lightning struck California's central coast and the inland Santa Lucia Mountains of Los Padres National Forest that form the watershed for the Carmel River. In shearing white, jagged electrical charges, the lightning pierced anything in its path, including the earth's achingly dry, thin crust of duff. Hot tributaries darted out from white-heat sources in the sky and painted their way through the blue darkness before angling faintly off at the horizon or heading straight downward, parallel to the mother bolt. The lightning blew the sky wide open and illuminated everything for an eternal instant, and everyone within its glow counted one thousand one, one thousand two, one thousand three.

Sample borings of trees on 5,860-foot Junipero Serra Peak near the southeastern boundary of the Ventana Wilderness show that for more than a hundred years, from 1790 to 1901, the trees burned six or seven times, and on the average, at about twenty years apart. However, from 1906 to 1999, there were an estimated 839 fires in the northern portion of Los Padres National Forest—an increase in fire frequency directly related to the increase in the neighboring population density. Most of these fires were caused by human carelessness and were usually easily contained, but the area quickly developed a reputation as one of the most fire-prone forests in the entire national forest system. Ninety-one fires in that same time span were started by lightning. In fact, fires burning the most acreage in 1977, 1985, and

1999 were all caused by lightning. There has not been a major lightning-caused fire in the last century that did not threaten the Carmel River watershed and virtually panic the water overseers. It is lightning, and not humans, that has historically inflicted the most damage on the watershed.

Back in 1916—on September 5, to be precise—the worst fire the country had ever seen burned out of control on a ridge between Big Sur and the upper reaches of the Carmel River. "Frantic efforts are being made to stem the huge forest fire which is spreading rapidly toward the headwaters of the Carmel River and imperiling the Carmel watershed, the saving of which is deemed so necessary to the future supply of the Monterey Peninsula," cried the *Monterey Daily Cypress*. The fire, just as was the one in 1999, was started by a lightning storm. Trees were burning on a ridge summit that was separated by only a narrow gulch from the river's headwaters. Firefighters gave the watershed a one-in-a-hundred chance of being saved if the flames jumped the gulch. C. S. Olmstead, superintendent of Monterey County Water Works, the private water company owned by the Del Monte Properties Company, tried to recruit volunteer firefighters and warned that if the fire swept through the watershed, not only would the Monterey Peninsula's supply of water be threatened but Carmel Valley would be in danger of flooding during the coming winter. His pleadings were so unsuccessful that district forest ranger Perry Hill had to telegraph Fort Baker in San Francisco for help from the army. The fire burned for eight days before it was contained, and credit for saving the Carmel watershed went to twenty soldiers with the First Company, 146th Coast Artillery Corps.

Late in the summer of 1924, a series of fires again struck the forest. A fire burned at Martin's Flat and another jumped the Carmel River near Pine Ridge. There was a fire on the Palo Colorado, another on Rocky Creek, another on Palo Corona Ridge, and another was burning near San Clemente Dam. Although an early October rain washed out the two smaller fires at Palo

Colorado and Rocky Creek, the other fires continued to grow. Fewer than seventy-five men were joined by a band of ranchers, but they were not enough. Firefighters from town were being recruited. Frank DeAmaral and his crew from the Carmel Development Company patrolled the coastal hills above the Highlands Inn watching for signs of fire coming in that direction.

"I took Frank Devendorf's men and supplies up to the day camp above the Highlands," DeAmaral recalled years later. "We used horses to haul the men up to the fire. There were eight or ten men. They had been fighting the fire for days and then on Sunday morning it clouded up and started to rain. It was like a godsend."

The fire burned for forty days, and whenever it appeared that the fire was about to be stopped a change of wind whipped it up again. It was only when the fire, which had burned a thirty-mile-long swath of the forest, was into its sixth week that thirty-one-hundredths of an inch of rainfall finally stalled it out, but the damage had been done. So much lye washed down the Carmel River and backed up at the San Clemente Dam in the winter following the 1924 fires that, as a precaution, the reservoir was completely drained after the first runoff so the contaminated water could escape before the winter's rains were stored for domestic use.

From the late 1920s to the mid-1970s the Carmel River watershed was in constant threat of fire. During that fifty-year period there were approximately five hundred fires in the U.S. Forest Service's Los Padres–Monterey District. The vast majority of these fires were caused by humans. Very few fires were started by lightning during that half-century, but the statistics were about to change.

In the mid-1970s three historic acts of nature united to create the second largest fire ever to burn in Los Padres National Forest, a fire that would destroy thousands of acres of watershed vegetation and once again threaten the Monterey Peninsula water supply. In 1974 an unusual snowstorm crushed and killed brush and trees over a two-hundred-thousand-acre area of the Santa Lucia Mountains. This came after one of the worst two-year droughts on record parched the area with less than half the "normal" rainfall. The year 1976 was the third driest in California's history, and 1977 was the driest—ever. And then, at 3:39 in the afternoon of August 1, 1977—in the middle of the worst drought in the history of the state—Mother Nature slapped a lightning storm over the reeling forest and sparked four fires. Two of the fires were put out before they could spread, but the other two fires quickly burned into one. The two fires became the infamous Marble-Cone Fire.

So much fuel had built up on the ground over the years, and was added to by the piling up of dried debris from crushed brush and trees caused by the 1974 snowstorm, that when the lightning hit, the trees and six-foot-high brush couldn't withstand it. The U.S. Forest Service gauged the fuel load at forty to fifty tons an acre. One acre released the same amount of energy as 5,800 gallons of gasoline. A thousand acres with this fuel load had the equivalence of a Hiroshima atomic bomb, and it was exploding near the headwaters of the Carmel River.

The Marble-Cone Fire raged for three weeks before it was surrounded by firebreaks. It was finally contained and burned itself out, but 177,900 acres, or 279 square miles, of the forest, including 93 percent of the Ventana Wilderness, birthplace of the Carmel River, had been destroyed. An estimated 18 percent, or 28,000 acres, of the Carmel River watershed had burned. Although there was no definitive data on the fire's impact on the steelhead population in the river, it was predicted that it would take ten years for fish life in the streams and creeks to return to their pre–Marble-Cone Fire numbers.

In the fire's aftermath, the U.S. Forest Service geared up for the longest running, most intensive and expensive rehabilitation of a burned-out forest ever undertaken in California. It spent $1.65 million over three years clearing the land of fallen trees, cleaning up 116 miles of rivers and streams, constructing check dams, and the unfortunate but apparently naïve replanting by hand and from c119 transport planes of 156,000 acres with one million pounds of nonnative annual rye (*Lolium*). A postfire study for the U.S. Forest Service by Jim Griffin, a research botanist at Hastings Natural History Reservation, University of California–Berkeley, discovered that the use of this aggressive, nonnative rye grass excluded all the recovery of native plants and left a sterile, vast expanse of understory—usually that lower level of vegetation in a forest, such as small trees and shrubs, but in this case dominated by only one species: rye. Scientists considered it the killing blow to a forest that had already been transformed into a moonscape of gray, smoking holes in the ground where the fire's heat had deeply penetrated the deep roots of trees and brush. In effect, the ecological clock had been set back to "start."

Damage to the Carmel River watershed was difficult to assess. There was extensive fire damage, but the coming winter rains could also add to the toll. Eventual estimates of watershed damage fell victim to complex bureaucratic formulas relying on the cost of reseeding and flood prevention measures, potential downstream damage, the amount of water runoff, siltation, land loss, and the type of vegetation destroyed. A more tangible measure of the damage is that in the following 1978 rain season, Los Padres Dam lost approximately 20 percent of its design storage, or nearly six hundred acre feet of its original three-thousand-acre-foot capacity, to silt spilling into the reservoir from the scarred and unprotected mountainsides of the watershed. During a seventy-two-hour period ending Monday, January 16, 1978, over five inches of rain fell at Los Padres Dam. With the runoff came a thick veneer of ash that floated on top of the reservoir's surface, a gray-black, bubbly froth. Further downstream and below San Clemente Dam sat Camp Steffani, originally a summer-cabin subdivision carved out of a larger ranch. Camp Steffani, perched on the banks of the river, had gradually evolved into a year-round settlement, and during the winter of

1978 its residents stood on their decks and watched the mass of debris rush by. Leslie Doolittle, born and raised in Carmel and living at Camp Steffani, was a witness.

"Our deck extended over the bank of the river and the water came up under it at times," he recalled. "After the fire, the first thing that happened was that many cords of firewood, which had been cut and piled in the riverbed upstream, floated by our house. For days on end we watched as logs, whole trees, and cut firewood roared by on the swollen river. I put plywood over the sliding doors and we crossed our fingers."

The cords of firewood Doolittle witnessed coming down the flood-stage river had been cut in the upper watershed to prevent debris dams of logs from forming and were in small rounds so they would easily flow with the river's current.

Not far downstream from Camp Steffani a large crowd of onlookers waited in the Robles del Río neighborhood to see if the river would overlap Rosie's Bridge. Meanwhile, William "Rosie" Henry, the owner of Rosie's Cracker Barrel on the lower, south side of the bridge, scoffed at reports his store would go under.

"I've been here thirty-nine years and I've never seen the water reach our door yet," he said. He remained dry, but the river rose ten feet while men from the county public works department used rappelling hooks to remove the logs and debris that snagged under the bridge.

Carmel's school superintendent wasn't as nonchalant as Henry. Warned that the river would crest on Monday afternoon, Harris A. Taylor sent all students home early, explaining that about 75 percent of the three thousand children in the school district rode the school bus. Not all the kids went home. Some went to the Highway 1 bridge where they stood and watched the rushing water hit the eighteen-foot marker, just nine inches short of the all-time high watermark set on Christmas Eve of 1955. A California highway maintenance crew probably saved the bridge when they managed to extract a thirty-five-foot tree trunk that had snagged on the bridge's supports. The river was on a roll.

Most of the flood damage in Carmel Valley was in riverbank erosion. Local property owners, who in the past were reluctant to tax themselves in order to support riverbank protection work by the U.S. Army Corps of Engineers, now spent thousands of dollars trying to halt further erosion. Ironically, the 1978 flooding of the Carmel River was equivalent to a ten-year flood; it wasn't even close to the feared standard of a hundred-year flood. There were three times during the storm period when one more inch of rain would have produced disastrous results, but each time the rain stopped.

"It was like somebody had a hand on the faucet," a county official remarked. "We really lucked out."

That summer, in early August, U.S. Forest Service District Ranger Bob Breazeale, invited a small group of journalists to take a helicopter tour of the burn area to see how the forest was recovering. A year had passed since the lightning strikes had ignited and burned nearly all of the Ventana Wilderness and a significant amount of the Carmel River watershed. What they saw was a forest attempting to rehabilitate itself, the invasive rye giving the appearance of a thriving grass cover. Tall green pines, formerly among heavy growth stands, were now mixed sparsely with brown and dead ones. In the forest's Los Burros mining district a sprinkling of wildflowers never seen before in that area sprouted up through gray ash. The indomitable poison oak was back. The burned oaks would leaf again if the cambium was intact. Wildlife, deer, upland game birds, and rodents that had escaped the fire were returning to what occasional water supplies they could find. Trout in the south fork of the Big Sur River were reported to be doing reasonably well; the water temperatures were cold enough but the sedimentation was restricting fish food supplies. It was obvious that the forest's recovery should not be taken for granted, and Breazeale made an ominous prediction. The Wilderness Act of 1964 desperately needed amending to allow prescribed burning in the Ventana; without controlled burning to reduce the heavy fire load of brush and debris accumulated with each passing year, Mother Nature would repeat herself and the next fire would be even more disastrous.

"The Los Padres region in twenty-eight years will be ecologically prime for another Marble-Cone Fire," he predicted, "and to stop its spread quickly will be impossible if as little as ten acres of land ignite."

In February 1978 President Jimmy Carter signed Public Law 95-237 providing for fire and watershed protection, or prescribed burning, in two wilderness areas, including the Ventana Wilderness. Fourteen years later, on June 19, 1992, President George H. W. Bush signed Public Law 102-301, the Los Padres Condor and River Protection Act, providing for fire prevention and watershed protection. In the twenty-one-year span from 1978 to 1999, even though provided for by federal law, there had never been a prescribed burn in the Ventana Wilderness. The reasons for this absence of controlled burning are as incredibly bizarre as they are complex. In the preparation of the National Fire Management Analysis System (NFMAS), which in part allocates budget and equipment to the Monterey District of Los Padres, mathematical errors were made in estimating budget items. The arithmetic was done by hand rather than by calculator, and no one double-checked the work. Firefighting items instantly disappeared from requisition lists because they weren't supported by the error-ridden budget. Los Padres National Forest also added a prescribed burn program to the budget mix, the only national forest to recommend prescribed burning under the new law, and that "threw off the numbers even more," said a U.S. Forest Service official. "We should never have done that." The Monterey District budget was slashed by more than half. Firefighter numbers and equipment dropped dramatically to about 41 percent of what they had been, well below their most effective level. Simultaneously, opposition to prescribed burning came from various environmental groups and eventually included the Monterey Bay Unified Air Pollution Control District. The Monterey District of Los Padres National Forest never recovered.

The lightning that started late September 8, 1999, lasted all that night. In the early darkness, people awestruck by the rare display across the sky drove to the beaches, to the ridge tops, anywhere they could see the show from a safe but thrilling seat. Professional photographers and anyone with an Instamatic were taking pictures. Up on Laureles Grade, high above the Carmel River, the winding two-lane road that connects the Salinas-Monterey Highway to Carmel Valley Road, one car after another stopped at the only wide turnout until there were fifteen to twenty cars and no room for another. And with each lightning strike on the western horizon they cheered. Nature was setting off a grand display of fireworks—the average flash could light a hundred-watt light bulb for more than three months—and the gallery, at its comfortable distance, spontaneously gasped and oohed and aaahed at each spectacular, pyrotechnic bolt that crashed toward earth. In Cachagua Valley, where the Carmel River winds its way toward the Pacific Ocean, the storm was an all-night bombardment. Lightning flashed unbelievably white and thunder instantly rolled down the valley.

Twenty-two years had passed since the Marble-Cone Fire, and the Monterey District of the Los Padres National Forest was severely underequipped for another big fire. To make matters worse from a firefighting perspective, the boundaries of the Ventana Wilderness—where motorized equipment is forbidden—had been expanded. There were only 22 full-time firefighters and one part-timer, instead of the 110 firefighters of 1977. There were only three fire engines, down from twelve, and no helicopters, no air tankers. The numbers were all it took to give Stephen Davis, the U.S. Forest Service's "incident commander" in charge of fighting fires, a feeling of dread as the lightning strikes came down. He was seriously outmanned if the forest started burning.

And it did.

By the time the storm passed at least 418 lightning strikes had touched down in Monterey County; the most lethal of the bolts penetrating the dry surface of Los Padres National Forest in fourteen vulnerable places—not far, as fire travels—from the Carmel River watershed. The fourteen lightning strikes ignited more fires in the Monterey District of Los Padres National Forest than at any time in six of the previous eight decades. Only two lightning-caused fires had occurred in the Monterey District of Los Padres National Forest since 1977. One was in winter and did not spread, and the other was quickly suppressed. Because there was no prescribed burning, the ground fuels had matured for more than twenty years, readying themselves for the ignition of a forest inferno that could exceed the Marble-Cone Fire and make Breazeale's prophetic prediction come true: A fire more than ten acres in size would be impossible to stop.

Large-scale fires started by indiscriminate lighting strikes, such as the 1999 fire in Los Padres National Forest, were oblivious not only to the Carmel River watershed that lay in its path but to state and local politics. And this fire could not have been more politically ill timed. After the passage, in 1978, of California's People's Initiative to Limit Property Taxation, known as Proposition 13, there was a growing antigovernment attitude and distrust of government policies and procedures developing nationwide. Proposition 13 had no direct relation to firefighting costs; even so, by 1999 there was a widespread watchdog populace looking over the government's shoulder and monitoring its spending practices, including how much the U.S. Forest Service spent on firefighting.

Davis had never heard of Breazeale's prediction, but he intuitively knew it to be true. He knew the potential damage a large fire would bring to the Carmel River, not necessarily in burned vegetation but in siltation to the reservoirs behind the Los Padres Dam and the downstream San Clemente. He knew there could be huge environmental problems coupled with the costs in controlling it, and he was thinking to himself, it's not so much that the forest isn't supposed to burn, it's the impact a big fire will have on an unprepared and skeptical community. He knew a fire would denude the watershed, erosion would result, and highways would be closed. In his mind, the people in the towns that got their water from the Carmel River watershed didn't understand the risk, the danger to the dams, to the roads, and to their homes. Cal-Am understood, but the public did not realize the potential danger and impact the fire could have on the Carmel River. People were out of touch with where their water came from and how it was delivered to them. This is what Davis was thinking when the U.S. Forest Service dispatcher in San Luis Obispo asked him, How bad is it?

"We have two six-hundred-acre fires going on that will just roar out of there," Davis told the dispatcher. He knew, as had happened with the Marble-Cone Fire, that in six hours, a fire, depending on a combination of wind, fuel, and type of terrain, can travel nine miles along a mile-long front.

Davis divided the fire area into different management teams, deployed his firefighters into position, and called in the Crew 7 firefighters out of Cal Poly–San Luis Obispo, California. Massive air power would be needed, and also a helicopter staging area at Carmel Valley and Tassajara Roads, the same location used in the 1977 Marble-Cone Fire. But the first staging would be Chews Ridge, overlooking the Carmel River watershed, and by the time Davis got up there the lightning strikes were pounding the forest. There was no rain and there was no immediate support from the California Department of Forestry because it was fighting fires to the north. Knowing that the Carmel River watershed had to be protected as much as possible, Davis decided to make a direct attack on the fires by using an existing trail system. The Carmel River Trail had just been reopened that year, so it was used as a fire line. But one of the first things needed were bulldozer operators experienced in working in tough backcountry, and he asked himself how he was going to break through all the bureaucratic crap to order them, to get permission to use bulldozers in a designated wilderness. Someone could get killed back there.

Davis was on the fire front forty-eight straight hours without a break. In the first two days he had managed to assemble 135 firefighters, seven engines, and two helicopters. On his way back to the forestry station, located on the river below the Los Padres Dam, he ran into a local television reporter.

"Why is there any worry about a fire in the backcountry?" she asked.

"Because it's not going to stay in the wilderness," Davis simply replied. "There are a lot of downstream issues."

Under the press of time and the preoccupation with the fire, the pun was understandable if unintended. What he didn't say was that the Carmel River was in danger. If the fire burned hot enough and with enough force it could destroy the sensitive watershed, jump the Carmel River, and head toward an urban disaster. But that was the unimaginable: that a fire could actually threaten the safety of humans in their habitat—a safety that was implicit in the contract that went with living in paradise. The fires had been burning for over two days now and they were out of sight, out of mind, and virtually nonexistent to one of the only links between what was actually occurring inside the forest and an unknowing public—a television reporter who failed to see the potential impact of a fire heading for the watershed.

September 16, the start of the second week of the fire, brought no hope for containment. A blast of northwest winds fanned the Five and Tassajara Fires and within a day or so they burned together. Smokejumpers and hand crews tried to hold to the Pine Valley Trail, which lies about halfway between South Ventana Cone and the Carmel River. Prison inmates from Los Angeles were put on the fire line, but for security reasons they had to stay together and couldn't spread out to fight the fire. Davis sent a helicopter to the Arroyo Seco River, which takes its water from a separate and distinct watershed, but was ordered not to take any water from the Los Padres National Forest side of the river because there was environmental litigation over the habitat. If he used the water he could impact the steelhead or red-legged frogs whose population numbers were being monitored. Any disturbance to the study would give environmentalists an excuse to try to shut down the forest. To circumvent the quandary, Davis sent the helicopters to the opposite bank of the Arroyo Seco River, which was privately owned and not subject to the litigation, and took the water from there. With some irony, the fire that eventually reached the Carmel River watershed came from the direction of its neighbor to the southeast—the Arroyo Seco watershed, which feeds into the Salinas Valley.

Overnight the combined fires expanded to 16,931 acres, nearly ten times larger than the day before. The firefighting force doubled to 2,612.

The next five days were critical. The California Department of Forestry joined the U.S. Forest Service in a unified command to battle the fires. Still the Five and Tassajara Fires continued to spread toward the river, reaching into Miller Canyon, the last natural barrier between the forest, the river, and homes, as well as to the south. Indirect fire lines were being constructed and a large burnout, where fires are purposefully set inside the control line in order to clear up fuels, was planned. It was staged along Chews Ridge during the night and was successful. The Internet reports referred to the fires as "growing." The Tassajara Fire continued to expand in a northeasterly and southeasterly direction. A new fire, called Snake, was discovered north of the Mountain Fire in the Rattlesnake drainage. This was not far from the Carmel River and the reservoir at Los Padres Dam. A hotshot crew was called in to fight it. In two weeks, over thirty-two thousand acres had burned. Smoke from the fires was so thick at times that elementary schools in Carmel Valley were closed for a day and all the children sent home. Customers at the local market walked into the parking lot and caught whole leaves of *Ceanothus* in the drifting ash.

On September 22, Cal-Am held a press conference in a pasture at the intersection of Tassajara and Carmel Valley Roads in Cachagua. Bruce Emmens, U.S. Forest Service district ranger from King City, was present. The pasture was a temporary a heliport for as many as eight helicopters used in fighting the fire. A four-thousand-gallon portable water tank had been placed at one side of the field to lessen, the attending press was told, the impact on the rancher's land and "the agriculture." Linda Morris, Cal-Am's human resources manager, introduced Judith Almond, vice president and manager of Cal-Am, to a pod of reporters standing around with notepads. Almond told them the estimated use of Carmel River water from Los Padres Reservoir for fighting fire was nine acre feet, or nearly three million gallons of water. For comparison, a family of four typically uses about half an acre foot of water in a year.

"Hope it won't be applied to our allocation," she joked, referring to the California Water Resources Board's limitations on Cal-Am's water draw. She said there was no reason that water used for fighting the fire would impact Monterey Peninsula consumers. Less than 1 percent of the water at the reservoir was being used on the fires, she said. Allocation figures, Almond explained, were unrelated to the new proposed dam issue, and Cal-Am was coming to the end of its water year, which was October 1 to September 30 of each year. A press release quoted Almond as saying, "We are supporting the firefighting efforts through the use of our facilities, staff time, and water resources. In the meantime, our people are working hard to do their part so that the fires can be extinguished as soon as possible to protect the downstream resources." No further explanation was offered, but "downstream resources" were assumed to mean the Carmel River and its dams.

Emmens filled the statistical void.

"From day one Cal-Am has made the water pickup available,"

he said. "So far, as of September 22, which is today, one million gallons of water have been used from Los Padres Dam. We're taking about one hundred thousand to three hundred thousand gallons a day. As for the Carmel River watershed area, there are thirty-five thousand acres of it in the national forest, of that about 10 percent is involved, or in the fire now. This fire is of lesser intensity than Marble-Cone."

The group then drove up to the Los Padres Dam, where Almond said the original reservoir had a capacity for three thousand acre feet, but was only at fifteen hundred acre feet because of backed-up siltation from sources like the 1977 Marble-Cone Fire.

As the press contingent was driving out, a reporter asked about the water coming out of a small pipe just below the wooden-planked bridge that crossed the dam. The water was dribbling down the face of the dam into a little fore bay.

"What's that water for, coming out of the pipe?" he asked.

"That goes into the Carmel River," answered a Cal-Am official from the front seat.

"What for?"

"That's to keep the river flowing."

"Are you kidding? Have you seen the river lately? It's dry."

"That's why we want a new dam."

For the next four days the fire continued to burn toward the Carmel River as statistics on the Internet continued to climb. Over forty-thousand acres had burned. There were more than three thousand firefighters, one hundred and five engines, and twenty-seven helicopters fighting the fire. The weather was dry and warm.

The fire was slow in its advance as it gathered up energy for a rush at the containment line. Still, within a day, another thirteen thousand acres burned and the threat to the Carmel River was becoming more apparent as the fire spread through the watershed and toward the river's natural dividing line between wilderness and suburbia. The firefighting strategy was to use the upper Carmel River as a control line on the north end of the fire. Crews began cutting an access route to the river and using helicopters in "light on the land" tactics for starting burnout fires.

It was estimated that 20 percent of the Carmel River watershed had burned so far. A Cal-Am representative said 2.5 million gallons of water had been drawn from the Los Padres Reservoir. There was another report that as many as sixteen air tankers had been called into use from air attack bases in Fresno and Paso Robles.

In the first month of the fire a total of 85,544 acres were burned. As the fire became more controlled, the number of firefighters were reduced to 555, but what remained unknown, as it was with every fire to hit Los Padres National Forest in the last century, was the damage to the Carmel River watershed. In the short term, there was the obvious prediction that sedimentation would drain into the Los Padres Reservoir; just how much, no one knew. The amount would depend on the winter rains. The sedimentation would bring "floatable" material with the first storms—material black in color like ash and burned leaves. In the path of the sedimentation would be young steelhead and red-legged frogs. There would have to be reseeding, this time with local, genetically native grasses and not nonnative rye. The long-range weather forecast was for a "La Niña" weather pattern, which would mean less rain than average. The fire was calm, burning far longer than the hot, fast-traveling Marble-Cone Fire of 1977. This one was consciously taking its time, burning out brush, little trees, some big ones, sparing others along its path. It was as if the fire was gradually, methodically cleaning house, working its way over the forest floor and the river's watershed at its own controlled pace; clearing rubbish the only way it knows how, free of good conscience, ethics, moral principles, and political persuasions. All firefighting apparatus placed in its mosaic path was a minor inconvenience to this fire. The smoke was its way of venting its message, and the inversion layers were the message carriers to town, laying a pall over Frank Devendorf's village of Carmel and Charles Crocker's old Monterey.

This morning there is the smell of smoke and I know it is coming from the backfires lit on the ridge.

"That's good smoke, not bad smoke," I tell myself.

There is a toleration. I forget for a moment how much smoke I must be breathing. There is a gray-blue haze that blots out the mountain ridges and blurs the eye as it tries to decipher depth of field, but there is no depth of field. Like the first wave of a whiteout, the smoke screens out color and form to almost nothing. There is nothing in front of it, nothing in back of it, and in the great distances to the horizon there is nothing to either side but smoke. Toward Chews Ridge it looks like a nuclear winter: smoke-laden skies, blue air, and the cherry-red glow of the fire on the underbelly of the cloud cover. I can't get the usual land bearings of being able to see the ridge to the south or way back to the southeast. My orientation becomes central to myself and how far I can see, which sometimes is only as far as the barn a couple of acres away. The fire creates its own environment. There is an isolation of place, and I am separated from the river and the rest of the world that is outside this fire environment.

There is an anxiety watching the low-flying helicopters going over with canvas buckets trailing underneath, buckets that just moments ago were dipped into the reservoir behind Los Padres Dam, a reservoir fed by the river, its waters returning to quench a river-threatening fire. There is anxiety in watching the smoke, watching the way the wind is blowing, if it ever does, watching the sky to the east to see if any new weather is coming, watching the sky to the west and not seeing the usual mountains in front of us, looking at our swimming pool covered with black and white ashes. Yesterday little drops of rain mixed with larger white ashes fell from the sky, and in my mind I saw the two— light rain and white ashes—settling on the river's surface as it slowly moved out to the ocean. This morning a slight rain fell, giving the dust of the corral a topping of little dark spots that looked like freckles. Walking kicks up the dust and covers the spots. There was some thunder in the northern distance and a worried neighbor called to say she saw lightning. Everyone is watching out for each other. Now it's raining more, like a real summer rain. The weather turns cold, the weather turns hot. The sky crane helicopter with the missing tooth, that gap between the pilot's compartment and water tank with its hose hanging down, passes over me like a monster cricket badly in need of dental work heading for the fire just on the other side of our ridge and the river.

Day by day there is a private fear of the unknown. This goes to the psychological concept that when I can't see the fire there is a mental reaction to it that magnifies everything. The fear and the fire build in my mind. Every plume of smoke, every helicopter, the ashes and charred leaves falling to the ground and on the river, the smoke blotting out the sky, the orange-red glows in the distance mean the fire is getting closer and closer in my mind and it makes me anxious. It is impossible to know exactly what is happening to the river's watershed, and I think back to those idyllic times, those romantic times on the Carmel River, the summers of my youth when there was no threat of any kind to the river, that I knew of, and how perfect it all seemed at the time. Now, in another time, the fire and its threat to the river wears on me. At the fire meeting last night they showed us a five-minute silent video of the fire and there was a reassurance in just seeing the pictures, and for the moment the private fear was relieved. But the fire is still out there. After the video, people in the audience applauded.

"Thank you. That answered a lot of questions," one woman said.

"The video was very helpful. I'm okay now," said a man.

"It was nice to see the stars last night," said another woman.

The rain comes at about five this morning. Softly at first without a wind to push it. It comes in layers. From our open bedroom window I can hear the drops hitting the composition roof of our cabin. At first it's a quiet rain and each drop seems singular in its purpose. And in the background, rain hitting the leaves of the oak trees that grow over our back deck. This is a higher-pitched sound and faster; drops pelting hundreds, maybe thousands of little oak leaves. The two are in tune, one against the other's rhythm and beat. And then, as the rain increases, I hear a tinny sound, as if the raindrops have formed into streamlets of water that have gathered and are running off something unseen in the morning darkness and striking light metal. When I stop trying to listen, all I hear is rain. There isn't even the smell that comes with a fall rain hitting dry surfaces. But when I try again to separate the sounds, there they are. Each to itself, like the rain is of different components and without the others it is nothing. Just a passing rain that comes and goes in about an hour and a half. By daylight all that is left is a low-hanging mountain cloud and a ground dampness deeper than dew. I see where the horses rolled and walked away, kicking up the leftover summer dust from under the thin layer of raindrops. Today is the fiftieth day of the fire in the river's watershed.

EPILOGUE

The Kirk Complex Fire, as it became known, was not controlled until November 30, 1999. A total of 87,619 acres were burned, of which 48,136 acres—more than half the total area of the fire—were in the Carmel River watershed. It cost $72 million to eventually stop the burning. A postfire assessment by the U.S. Forest Service estimated that capacity of the reservoir behind Los Padres Dam—"the sole source of drinking water for the City of Carmel," and already seriously diminished by the 1977 Marble-Cone Fire—would be further reduced by 10 percent. Furthermore, there was a definite danger to the water quality of the Carmel River and its already threatened steelhead.

Since the Kirk Complex Fire, an estimated seven hundred acres per year are managed by "controlled" or prescribed burns, according to the U.S. Forest Service. "The Monterey District does not get a lot of support for burning from the local community," one U.S. Forest Service official explained. "All it takes is one landowner to say no, and a lot of planning goes to waste. The public gets tired of the environmental reviews and time it takes for reviews. Public support is there one minute, and gone the next. We do get some support, but most supporting groups lose interest due to the amount of time for reviews and other agency compliance."

In 1987 the Carmel River's public agency guardian, the Monterey Peninsula Water Management District (MPWMD), issued a study for managing the river. The study dealt with a variety of river subjects including sedimentation, channel erosion, loss of vegetation, flooding, habitat protection, and even the legal status of the Carmel Valley groundwater through which the river flows. Although the study was actually prepared for the California Department of Fish and Game as a "working paper" report, it served to identify the history of river habitat change brought about by both natural and human causes. It was a beginning in the attempt to resuscitate the Carmel River. In the intervening years there have been many other studies, but perhaps equally as important is a gradual public awareness of the river's plight. Various efforts have been made in restoring the river's eroded banks, recovering lost wetlands, and in managing its floodplains.

In 1992 the California Department of Water Resources' Division of Dam Safety declared the seventy-one-year-old San Clemente Dam unsafe. The Division of Dam Safety said the dam could collapse in a 5.5 earthquake on the Tularcitos Fault, which it straddles, or from a magnitude 7.0 earthquake on the San Andreas Fault. At the time that the state red-tagged the dam, its reservoir was at 90 percent capacity, containing 2.5 million cubic yards of sediment. That left the obvious question faced by all western U.S. dams planned or considered for removal: What do you do with the sediment? Cal-Am's answer was not to deal with the sediment behind the San Clemente Dam. Instead it responded to the state with a plan to strengthen or buttress the dam against future earthquakes. As expected, that suggestion did not meet with the approval of steelhead fishermen.

In 1999 the California Sportfishing Protection Alliance, based in Quincy, sent a letter to the U.S. Army Corps of Engineers in San Francisco, which was also working on its own plans for a new and larger San Clemente Dam. The Sportfishing Protection Alliance called the San Clemente a "useless dam" and opposed any retrofitting of the dam by Cal-Am. And in mid-2006 the U.S. Environmental Protection Agency's Region 9 office in San Francisco stated its concerns with Cal-Am's retrofit plan, which was endorsed by the U.S. Army Corps of Engineers and somewhat ironically by the California Department of Water Resources, and asked for more information.

Fourteen years after the state issued its warning that the San Clemente Dam was unsafe, the California Department of Water Resources in 2006 released a draft environmental impact report evaluating Cal-Am's buttressing plan plus four other options that included removal of the dam and rerouting of a section of the river where San Clemente Creek intersects the Carmel River. In 2007 the report was certified, and in 2008 a final statement was issued endorsing the reroute and removal alternative. Agencies working with Cal-Am in favor of the reroute and removal plan were the California Coastal Conservancy, the National Marine Fisheries Services, and the Planning and Conservation League Foundation. The Conservancy's role was to manage project planning and design, and with assistance from the National Marine Fisheries Services, coordinate with the regulatory agencies to secure all permits and "expeditious approval of the project."

Cal-Am was to manage the project construction, and after completion, transfer approximately 928 acres in the project area to the Monterey Peninsula Regional Park District for watershed conservation and compatible public access. The total project cost was estimated at $83 million. Cal-Am's share was $49 million, or an amount equal to the cost of buttressing the dam. The California State Coastal Conservancy, with assistance from the National Marine Fisheries Services, was to secure the additional $34 million from state, federal, and private foundation sources. The California State Coastal Conservancy said in approval, "the reroute and removal project—not buttressing—presented a unique opportunity for public interests to work together . . . and offered a permanent solution to the dam safety issue." The Conservancy, serving as the lead state agency, was also willing to put up $6 million for studies and permits.

And what about the 2.5 million cubic yards of sedimentation? In 2009 the solution to safely getting rid of the sediment lay in the rerouting of a half-mile section of the Carmel River and using the abandoned reach of the river as a disposal site. The rerouting required blasting a new channel through a ridge separating the river from San Clemente Creek and diverting the river into the creek just below the dam—a four-to-five-year project. At one point it was suggested that additional help could come from the U.S. Department of Defense's Innovative Readiness Training Program, where military reserves work on civilian projects.

But funding was suspended in 2009 when California's budget went into a spiraling turmoil. Money was frozen and stop-work orders were issued to contractors, including work on the San Clemente Dam project. Adding to the breakdown in progress was an announcement in February 2009 that San Clemente Dam would not be demolished after all, not just because of a deep freeze in state spending but because Cal-Am and the California Coastal Conservancy disagreed over the project's liability. The Conservancy did not want to take on liability during demolition or after the dam was removed from the river. Cal-Am rejected any notion that potential lawsuits be the responsibility of its ratepayers.

Then, in January 2010, the San Clemente Dam was back in the news with the announcement that Cal-Am and the California Coastal Conservancy had arrived at an agreement to go forward with its demolition. The question of liability was averted when it became apparent that Cal-Am, faced with potential lawsuits, would not be getting the necessary permits for repairing the dam from the National Marine Fisheries Service. "We have been telling Cal-Am that a project to buttress the dam would likely result in the fish becoming extinct," Fisheries Service central coast supervisor Joyce Ambrosius was quoted in news coverage of the agreement. She was, of course, referring to the steelhead population in the Carmel River. The impasse, according to news reports, was broken when a new Cal-Am president was named and Congressman Sam Farr, whose district includes the boundaries of the river, pressed for removal of the dam.

Initial plans for rerouting the river, keeping the sediment in the rerouted section instead of trucking it out, remain in place. Construction on the channel to temporarily reroute the river is projected to begin in 2013 and will take three years to complete. Costs of removing the dam remain at approximately $50 million, to be paid by Monterey Peninsula water users, and another $34 million coming from federal and state agencies. But, at the end of 2010, in late November and early December, the California Coastal Conservancy and the National Marine Fisheries Service jointly stated that if various permits were approved by the end of 2011, deconstruction of the dam could take place as early as 2012 and completed in 2015. Demolition of the 106-foot-tall San Clemente—when it actually does occur—may be the largest dam removal project ever undertaken in California. The largest dam to be removed in the state to date was the fifty-five-foot Sweasey Dam in Humboldt County in 1970, after its reservoir silted up. A 2004 plan to take down the 165-foot Matilija Dam in Ventura County, because it too filled with silt, has not been carried out because of lack of funding.

Entwined in this sequence of events is a 1995 order by the California Department of Water Resources Control Board that Cal-Am reduce water extraction from its twenty-one wells along the river in Carmel Valley by 20 percent and to stop unlawful diversions, either by obtaining additional water rights or by obtaining replacement water from other sources. The wells supply an estimated 69 percent of the water needs of Cal-Am's Monterey Peninsula customers. It was estimated at the time that Cal-Am was unlawfully extracting 10,730 acre feet per year. By the end of 2004 the Monterey Peninsula Water Management District reported that the issue was still under study by Cal-Am and no timeline for "completion of a water supply project is currently available."

On January 15, 2008, the California Department of Water Resources Control Board came back with an order that Cal-Am reduce its aquifer pumping in the Carmel River by 15 percent, followed by another 15 percent in 2009, with the illegal diversions of water ending in 2014. That order changed on July 27, 2009, when the Water Resources Control Board issued a new draft order requiring Cal-Am to reduce pumping by 5 percent within two months and continue smaller reductions each year until 2014. In issuing its latest order, the state noted in frustration, "Nearly fourteen years after the adoption of (the 1995) order, Cal-Am is unable to tell the state water board what project may be built to end its illegal diversions, when a project will be approved, or when construction might be commenced. Indeed, there is no assurance that any project will be approved during the next several years." In the meantime, the reservoir behind Los Padres Dam is at half capacity because of the filling in of sedimentation—only adding to the problem of Carmel River water supply heightened by the filling in of the San Clemente Dam reservoir. The Monterey Peninsula Water Management report estimated that Los Padres Reservoir will be completely filled with sediment in forty to fifty years and will have virtually no surface storage capacity.

On April 6, 2010, the answer the Water Resources Control Board was waiting for arrived when the Monterey County Board of Supervisors conditionally approved plans for a ten-million-gallon-per-day desalination plant, widely estimated to cost $280 million to $390 million—a cost that is expected to double ratepayers' water bills. The proposed plant, to be located at the north end of the Monterey Peninsula, must undergo a series of public hearings before the California Public Utilities Commission (CPUC). The CPUC is the lead agency under the California Environmental Quality Act for the desal proposal and regulates Cal-Am because it is an investor-owned public utility. If approved by the CPUC, the desal plant would operate under a public-private partnership in which the Monterey County Water Resources Agency would own wells from which brackish water would be drawn in the vicinity of the city of Marina, the Marina Coast Water District would own the desal plant, and

Cal-Am would build a ten-mile pipeline to deliver the water to its Monterey Peninsula customers. The project, while no timeline for its start or completion has been announced, could satisfy the Water Recourses Control Board's order that Cal-Am cutback its overdrafting of the Carmel River.

Approval of the desal proposal came from the CPUC on December 2, 2010, but it came with a price tag of $486 million and not the original estimate of $280 million to $390 million—and the price could go even higher. An analysis by the California Division of Ratepayer Advocates (CDRA) argues that Monterey Peninsula water users could pay up to $500 million in infrastructure, maintenance, and operation costs. If the $500 million figure is reached, the CDRA predicts desalinated water on the Monterey Peninsula will cost as much as $11,000 an acre foot, nearly four times what the most expensive desalinated water costs anywhere in the world. The CPUC rejected the CDRA's recommendation to cap project costs at a $2,200 an acre foot, which is in line with the California Department of Water Resources' range of costs for seawater desalination in California of $1,000 to $2,500 an acre foot. The CDRA, which supports the desal project in principle, is an independent consumer advocacy office housed within the California Public Utilities Commission.

Interestingly, the proposed desal plant is not within the boundaries of the Monterey Peninsula Water Management District, which has regulation authority over a Cal-Am pipeline bringing desalinated water into the MPWMD boundaries. At the time of the Monterey County Board of Supervisors' approval of a desal plant to be operated under a public-private partnership, there remained an unresolved "political" issue—the proposal effectively marginalizes the role of the MPWMD, which represents the interests of the very people who will be paying most of the water project bill.

As for the steelhead? In 2003–4 the MPWMD made an environmental and biological assessment of portions of the Carmel

River that confirmed that the steelhead count was below historic numbers for the Carmel River "and well below populations found in other Northern California coastal streams." There are multiple reasons for the poor numbers, according to the study: areas of the Carmel River are unsuitable for steelhead spawning, and riparian wetlands are "functionally impaired due to water extraction and development adjacent to the stream banks." The report noted that "the cumulative effect of human influences has resulted in a fragmented environment in the lower twenty-seven miles of the river that requires intensive management efforts . . . [and] regulation of water extraction from the basin is in effect under orders from the California Department of Water Resources and subsequent related orders." The study concluded that the fish are recovering. One reason for the low numbers, according to the report—four hundred to eight hundred fish—was the trap-and-truck operation at Los Padres Dam that requires that the fish be moved upstream in order to move them back downstream. To begin their migration to the ocean the fish that make it to the dam have to slide down a concrete spillway before dropping into the river. The other reason for the low numbers is an outdated fish ladder at San Clemente Dam, where fish plunge seventy feet over the dam's spillway to their death in the pool below—at least until the dam is removed from the river.

Is there relief in sight? Yes, momentum for saving the river has been growing slowly but steadily. Recognizing that community investment is the key to the Carmel River's resurrection, the Big Sur Land Trust, an advocate of open-space protection in various forms since 1978, released an ambitious Carmel River Valley Conservation Program in 2005 that—if carried out—will create a Carmel River Parkway.

"Many people don't realize that the Carmel River is a very significant river in California, with a long cultural and environmental history," said Donna Meyers, director of conservation programs for the Big Sur Land Trust. "Today, government and civic agencies struggle to find solutions that will provide the area with the water it needs while restoring and preserving the river and its inhabitants."

The Carmel River Valley Conservation Program is a twenty-five-year plan with a $40-million fundraising goal. Its intent is to restore the natural purpose of the Carmel River and in doing so reconnect the river to the local community. This includes the establishment of benchmarks such as the current health of the river. Factors including river flow, water quality, health and abundance of plants, fish and other river animals, and the vibrancy of wetlands and habitats will all be measured. A total of $7 million is projected for land purchases, easement agreements, trail construction and river restoration, landscape restoration, and preservation along the river, including restoring natural floodplains and replanting trees and native plants. Community investment also means partnering with existing organizations such as the Carmel River Steelhead Association and the Carmel River Watershed Conservancy in order to raise funds and gain widespread public involvement.

The concept of a Carmel River Parkway envisions an integrated trail and parkland system along the river, tying in with existing trails that lead to established regional and state parks, and even area schools, shopping centers, and businesses as part of an education and public awareness effort to reconnect people to the river. Another goal of the plan is to perpetuate the family ranching tradition in Carmel Valley by developing innovative, private landowner agreements that monetarily reward families who agree to continue that ranching tradition. The purpose of such easements will be the preservation of open space along the river. Toward that goal, the Big Sur Land Trust announced in 2006 the purchase of thirty-two acres along the river at a cost of $2.3 million, aided by a $1.9-million grant from the California State Resources Agency River Parkway Program.

The Carmel River no longer merely empties into Carmel Bay as it did when Sebastian Vizcaino discovered it in 1603. Today it empties into a state-designated "Area of Special Biological Significance" located within the federally protected Monterey Bay National Marine Sanctuary, which was formed in 1992. The sanctuary stretches 276 miles along the California coastline, from Marin County on the north to San Luis Obispo County to the south. This is where the Big Sur Land Trust has proposed a second plan for the river. The plan is called the Lower Carmel River and Lagoon Floodplain Restoration and Enhancement Project. It calls for the improvement of habitat and management of the river's lagoon on the west side of Highway 1, just south of Carmel, and restoring the floodplain on the east side of the highway. Related to this program are efforts by the California Department of Parks and Recreation. Using $4 million in funds from the California Coastal Conservancy, the state's Parks and Recreation Department has expanded the Carmel River lagoon by restoring agricultural land next to it. The project included reestablishing a long-dormant south arm of the lagoon for steelhead and riparian wildlife. Also, using funds from California's Integrated Regional Water Management Grant Program, the Big Sur Land Trust was able to complete the first stage of a floodplain modeling study of the lower Carmel River near the state parks project. The purpose of the study, according to the Big Sur Land Trust, is to identify various alternatives for future floodplain restoration.

Whether these plans, which rely heavily on state funding, are fully carried out is clouded by California's serious budget deficit. Additionally, a national economy in recession, as it was in 2010–11, does not favor nonprofits that rely on generous private contributions and endowments. Ambitious as these projects are, and as uncertain as they may be because of California's budget crisis, they are in the shadow of two major challenges on the river: one is the overdrafting of the river's aquifers and the other is a dam that has been declared virtually unsafe and still to be removed.

With one or two exceptions, this analysis may sound dreary and clinical: politics, emotions, and pragmatism are among the driving forces behind the recovery of the Carmel River—in some cases they have been hindrances to the river's future. But all in all, the attention now being given to the river's revival is a perfect example of "planning for our children's future"—especially in the instance of the ambitious and justifiably utopian hopes of the Big Sur Land Trust. The process of river restoration and eventual recovery is a slow one. Help for the river started to arrive when some people now in early adulthood were children. The results of that aid will no doubt come to some realization when their children are young adults. In a sense, the passage of time is irrelevant if the eventual outcome means the successful reincarnation of the river.

It's been written that water, and not wind, fire, humans, or gods, defines the land. What this means is that free-flowing water carves its way to its eventual destination, unhampered by any obstacles it may encounter in its path, and in doing so leaves its signature on the land. Water, contrary to the adage, does not necessarily take the path of least resistance. The Carmel River, any river, is water, and a less optimistic observer might argue that in the case of the Carmel River just the opposite has been true—that wind, fire, humans, and perhaps even the gods, have conspired to define its waters rather than the reverse. If that is true, that humans were the architects of the river's demise, which was clearly true of the river's ruin, then humans have the opportunity to redeem themselves.

The Monterey Peninsula can take back its river and, in embracing it, give the river new meaning by making it a living, pulsating vein that courses through the community as the integral and eternal lifeline we humans are so dependent on for our moral and physical existence.

ACKNOWLEDGMENTS

This is not an inflated metaphor: researching and writing this book has been like shooting the rapids of a wild river. One minute it's calm, serene, floating dreamlike, the next moment anxious, the roar of unseen rapids in the ear followed by certain fear, and then exhilaration, survival, and safety until it is repeated all over again until finally, exhausted, we beach.

I have not been the captain on this voyage, not even the necessary pilot. I've only been a passenger at the observation deck, making notes. The captain has been my wife, Barbara, a poet, publisher, and keen editor with credits far exceeding mine. I acknowledge her as the one person who guided me over the years it took to research and write this book.

Of course, even two people cannot possibly accomplish the necessary labor that goes into a project such as this. There have been many who were always there when I needed them. Namely, the highly regarded Dennis Copeland, Monterey Public Library archivist and overseer of the California History Room and Archives, who scoured the depths of his files whenever called upon; Nikki Nedeff who sat beside me that sunny day at the lagoon on February 21, 2002, and told me the river's history and then read draft after draft of the book making corrections, suggestions, and giving encouragement; as did Keith Vandevere, who knows the political side of the Carmel River better than anyone; and Stephen Davis of the U.S. Forest Service for his review of the Kirk Complex Fire account.

Special thanks to Jane Hohfeld Galante, who opened her Carmel Valley home and personal files of the Carmel Development Company to me and let me draw whatever I needed from them. And to Allene Fremier, now departed, who graciously and with her usual sense of good humor, shared the diary of Anne Nash. And, of course, there are my high school classmates who looked back those many years with great fondness for the Carmel River: Cherie Staples, Alice Barr, Del Meyer, and the late Les Doolittle.

My particular thanks goes to Matt Bokovoy of the University of Nebraska Press, who appeared out of nowhere, to guide me through the process of giving the book more depth, credibility, and substance. It was Bokovoy who saw the early promise in a rough draft and shepherded the book through the peer review maze. His editing skills are the trench work that too often goes unnoticed, but not by this writer.

Belle Yang, Steve Turner, John Walton, Gerald Haslam, and Malcolm Margolin read and commented on parts or all of various early drafts. My appreciation goes out to them all. Of course, I am responsible for the final version.

There are so many others who gave their time, knowledge, and patience, including Jack Galante, Robert R. Curry, Thomas Christensen, Mark Stromberg, Graham Matthews, Fred Nason, Sandy Lyon, Kevan Urquhart and many expert staffers at the Monterey Peninsula Water Management District. If I omitted someone, I apologize, hoping they know how much I appreciate their support, both moral and material.

There are also the unknown contributors, those journalists, many times without by-lines, who over the years wrote unsparingly about the river for their respective newspapers. I am the beneficiary of your work. Thank you all for your insights, your diligence, and your courage in reporting a story as it was being unveiled.

A work of this kind is never the work of one person.

SELECTED BIBLIOGRAPHY

This book, written over a period of many years, is based on both my personal observations as a career journalist and research in the history of water in California, most specifically the Monterey Peninsula. It would have been impossible to complete this work had it not been for the numerous scholars who have so meticulously studied and written on a variety of subjects covering not only Monterey's unique locale but also California and the West. On the surface it would appear that these various works are unrelated, but on close examination there is almost always a common thread or clue that leads to information useful in forming conclusions or just simple observations necessary in writing the story of the Carmel River. The common thread is often the similarities between California rivers at a given time—the almost eerie coincidence that a river remote from the Carmel River is suffering the same fate at exactly the same time.

Of particular note, although not specifically listed in this bibliography, are the many newspapers used as resources that reflected not only the on-the-scene descriptions of dams and hotel construction but also the social and political environment of the various periods covered in this work. Examples are early issues of the *Carmel Pine Cone, Monterey Daily Cypress, Monterey Daily Herald, Monterey Californian, Monterey Cypress, Monterey Gazette, Monterey Weekly Argus, Monterey Trader, Pacific Grove Progress,* and *San Francisco Chronicle.* The *Monterey Peninsula Herald,* which later evolved into the *Monterey County Herald,* was especially rich in source material.

The research and writing of this book was also dependent on other, nonprofessional sources, such as resident activists who have a vested interest in the future and environmental well-being of the Monterey Peninsula and Carmel River. Of equal significance is the historic richness of the area. Without the recording of Monterey's discovery, founding, and political role in forming the state of California there would not be the vast resource of material available in such repositories as the Monterey Public Library's California History Room and Archives, where much of my research took place. This bibliography, then, provides only a limited overview of the research necessary to accomplish this book, a necessary guideline in forming a foundation for reliable information about the development of the Monterey Peninsula and its reliance on the Carmel River. There was much material that was not used as direct sources, but rather for educational or background purposes, some of which is included here. However, to list all these resources or even to include the use of footnotes would, in my opinion, have made for a work of awkward and disrupting proportions.

UNPUBLISHED SOURCES

Barr, Alice. Correspondence with the author, October 12, 2001.
Bernardi, Pat. E-mail correspondence with the author, January 20, 2010.
Bowie, Catherine (Cal-Am Manager of External Affairs). E-mail correspondence with the author, May 20, 2009.
Breazeale, Bob (Senior Fellow, Pinchot Institute). Interview by the author, December 6, 2001.
"California Central Valley Steelhead DPS," NOAA's National Marine Fisheries. Date Listed: August 18, 1997 (62 FR 43937). Endangered status reaffirmed January 5, 2006. http://www.nmfs. (Note: DPS stands for District Population Segments).
California Railroad Commission. Case no. 1756. Carmel Development Company files. Courtesy of Jane Hohfeld Galante.
California Water Code Sections 6250–6253 and 6380–6382.
Carmel Development Company files. Courtesy of Jane Hohfeld Galante.
Carmel River Restoration Program. File no. 02-090. Project Manager: Neal Fishman. Coastal Conservancy, October 25, 2003.
Carmel River Watershed Management Plan. Vol. 2. Monterey Peninsula Water Management District, January 1987.
Christensen, Thomas. Telephone interview with the author, April 14, 2008.

Curry, Robert. "The Story of the Carmel River." Presentation by the Carmel River Watershed Council, February 7, 2001.

Davis, Steve (U.S. Forest Service Fire Prevention Officer). Interviews and briefings provided to the author, undated.

DeAmaral, Frank, and Mrs. Frank (Lillian) Devendorf. Tape recording, 1971. Courtesy of Jane Hohfeld Galante.

"Deliveries, Monterey Bay Area." Charts provided by the Monterey Fish Processors Association, California History Room, Monterey Public Library.

Dobbins, John (Electronic Resources Librarian, Occidental College Library). E-mail correspondence with the author, April 18, 2007.

Doolittle, Leslie. Correspondence with the author, November 16, 2001.

Environmental and Biological Assessment of Portions of the Carmel River Watershed. Monterey Peninsula Water Management District, December 2004. Available from the district office in Monterey CA.

Galante, Jack. Correspondence with the author, undated.

Global Atmospherics, Inc. Correspondence with the author, January 4, 2000.

Hare, Lou G. Personal diaries, 1883–1929. Transcribed by Lou Frost, California History Room, Monterey Public Library.

History Chart. City Hall, City of Carmel-by-the-Sea CA.

"Instream Flow Needs for Steelhead in the Carmel River." National Marine Fisheries Service, Santa Rosa CA office, June 3, 2002. Available at http://www.swr.nmfs.noaa.gov.

Lagorio, Elmer (Pebble Beach Company archivist). Telephone interview with the author, undated.

Lent, Rebecca, Ph.D. National Marine Fisheries Service letter to Monterey Peninsula Water Management District, May 24, 2001.

Lydon, Sandy (Author of *Chinese Gold: The Chinese in the Monterey Bay Region*). Correspondence with the author, September 11, 2002.

Matthews, Graham. Correspondence with the author, March 1, 2005.

McLendon, Rose (Harrison Memorial Library, Carmel CA, History Room). Correspondence with the author, July 14, 2008.

Nash, Anne. Personal diaries, 1921 and 1922. Courtesy of Allene Fremier.

Nason, Fred. Conversation with the author, March 6, 2003.

Meyer, Del. Correspondence with the author, 2001.

Monterey Pharmacy Registers, 1876–1914. [Vol. 2], California History Room and Archives, Monterey Public Library.

Nedeff, Nicole. Correspondence with the author, November 3, 2000, November 13, 2001, March 13, 2003, January 17, 2010.

Russell, Helen Crocker. Correspondence to Mrs. James (Jean) Dickie, December 16, 1963, and undated. Harrison Memorial Library, Park Branch, Carmel CA.

Sanders, John (Deputy Public Affairs Officer, Naval Postgraduate School). Correspondence with the author, May 14, 2002, and telephone interview, May 13, 2002.

Scrivani, Lawrence. "The First Century and a Half of Newspaper Publishing in Monterey County: A Survey of the Historic Newspapers of Monterey County from 1846 to 2006." Pacific Grove CA: Unpublished manuscript, 2008.

Stanford University Special Collections. Pacific Improvement Company Records, 1869–1931.

Staples, Cherie. Correspondence with the author, October 11, 2001.

Steinbeck, John. Correspondence with the author, January 3, 1963.

"The Story of the Carmel River Watershed." Brochure produced by RisingLeaf Watershed Art, undated.

Stromberg, Mark R., Ph.D. (Resident Manager, Hastings Natural History Reservation, University of California-Berkeley). Correspondence with the author, December 2, 1999, and May 10, 2002.

Thomas, Tim (Museum Historian/Curator, Monterey Maritime History Museum). Correspondence with the author, April 15, 2009.

Urquhart, Kevan (Senior Fisheries Biologist, Monterey Peninsula Water Management District). E-mail correspondence with the author and telephone interview, April 17, 2007.

U.S. Forest Service. *Arroyo Seco Watershed Analysis*, August 2000. Available from the USFS Monterey Ranger District office, Los Padres National Forest, King City CA.

———. "Kirk Complex BAER (Burned Area Emergency Report)," November 20, 2001. Available from the USFS Monterey Ranger District Office, Los Padres National Forest, King City CA.

———. "Management Plan—Los Padres National Forest," 1988. Working Paper available from the USFS Supervisor's office, Los Padres National Forest, Goleta CA.

————. Final Environmental Impact Statement, Land and Resource Management Plan. Los Padres National Forest (California Room, Monterey City Library).

U.S. National Marine Fisheries Service. SW Region letter, October 10, 1997. Available from the NMFS, Southwest Region, Santa Rosa CA.

Vandevere, Keith. Correspondence with the author, March 1, 2003, and November 8, 2007.

————. *Water Over The Dam*. Carmel CA: Unpublished manuscript, copyright 1998.

WPA Historical Survey of the Monterey Peninsula. Project no. 4080, File 108, July 28, 1937. California History Room Archives, Monterey Public Library, Monterey, California.

PUBLISHED SOURCES

Bancroft, Hubert Howe. *History of California, 1860–1890* Vol 24, *The Works of Hubert Howe Bancroft*. San Francisco: The History Company, 1890.

Barter, Eloise Richard. *The French Potter of Monterey*. Sacramento: California State Parks, 2003.

Big Sur Land Trust. "A River Runs Through Us: The Big Sur Land Trust Unveils Carmel River Valley Conservation Program." *Big Sur Land Trust Newsletter*, Fall 2006.

Blakley, E. R. (Jim), and Karen Barnette. "Historical Overview of Los Padres National Forest." U.S. Forest Service, July 1985.

Boyle, Robert H., John Graves, and T. H. Watkins. *The Water Hustlers*. San Francisco: Sierra Club, 1971.

Brewer, William H. *Up and Down California in 1860–1864*. Berkeley: University of California Press, 1966.

Brown, William S. "History of the Los Padres National Forest—1898–1945." Goleta CA: USDA, Forest Service, Los Padres National Forest, 1945.

"California's Living Marine Resources: A Status Report." Sacramento CA: California Department of Fish and Game, December 2001.

Cannon, Lou. "High Dam in the Valley of the Tall Grass." *The New Book of California Tomorrow*. Edited by John Hart. Los Altos CA: William Kaufmann, 1984.

Chiang, Connie Y. *Shaping the Shoreline: Fisheries and Tourism on the Monterey Coast.* Seattle: University of Washington Press, 2008.

Childs, Craig. *The Secret Knowledge of Water.* Boston: Little, Brown and Company, 2000.

Carruth, Gorton. *The Encyclopedia of American Facts and Dates.* 8th ed. New York: Harper & Row, 1987.

Clark, Donald Thomas. *Monterey County Place Names.* Carmel Valley CA: Kestrel Press, 1991.

Culleton, James. *Indians and Pioneers of Old Monterey.* Fresno: Academy of California Church History, 1950.

Entrix Environmental Consultants. *San Clemente Dam Seismic Project.* Draft Environmental Report/Environmental Impact Statement prepared for the California Department of Water Resources and U.S. Army Corps of Engineers on behalf of Cal-Am, April 2006.

Folger, Tim. "Requiem for a River." *On Earth,* Spring 2008.

Ford, Tirey L. *Dawn of the Dons: The Romance of Monterey.* San Francisco: A. M. Robertson, 1926.

Gilliam, Harold, and Ann Gilliam. *Creating Carmel—The Enduring Vision.* Layton UT: Gibbs Smith, 1992.

Gilmore, R. M. *Why Southern Pacific Finds It Necessary to Discontinue the Del Monte.* Southern Pacific Railroad, pamphlet, 1962.

Gumprecht, Blake. *The Los Angeles River: Its Life, Death, and Possible Rebirth.* Baltimore: The Johns Hopkins University Press, 1999.

Heimann, Richard F. G., and John G. Carlisle Jr. "The California Marine Fish Catch for 1968 and Historical Review 1916–1968." *Fish Bulletin* no. 149 (California Department of Fish and Game), 1970.

Jeffers, Robinson. *The Selected Poetry of Robinson Jeffers.* New York: Random House, 1959.

Jeffers, Robinson, and Horace Lyon. *Jeffers Country: The Seed Plots of Robinson Jeffers' Poetry.* San Francisco: Scrimshaw Press, 1971.

Keeley, Jon E., C. J. Fotheringham, and M. Morais. "Reexamining Fire Suppression Impacts on Brushland Fire Regimes." *Science* 284, no. 5421 (June 11, 1999): 1829–32.

Kondolf, G. Mathias, and Robert B. Curry. "Channel Erosion along The Carmel River, Monterey County, California." *Earth Surface Processes and Landforms* 11, no. 3 (May/June 1986): 307–19.

Lewis, Oscar. *The Big Four*. New York: Alfred A. Knopf, 1938.

Lydon, Sandy. *Chinese Gold: The Chinese in the Monterey Bay Region*. Capitola CA: Capitola Book Company, 1985.

March, Ray A. *A Guide to Cannery Row*. Monterey CA: privately printed, 1962.

———. *A Paradise Called Pebble Beach*. Trumbull CT: Golf Digest/ Tennis, 1992.

Mathes, Michael W. *Vizcaino and Spanish Expansion in the Pacific Ocean, 1580–1630*. San Francisco: California Historical Society, 1968.

McEwan, Dennis, and Terry A. Jackson. *Steelhead Restoration and Management Plan for California*. Sacramento: California Department of Fish and Game, February 1996.

Monterey County, Resources, Advantages, and Prospects. Oakland and San Francisco: E. S. Harrison, 1889.

Monterey Peninsula Water Management District. *How to Protect & Enhance Your Property along the Carmel River*. Monterey CA: MPWMD, 1995–96.

———. *Information for Land Owners Proposing Works in the Carmel River*. Monterey CA: MPWMD, Winter–Spring 1981.

Moritz, Max A. "Analyzing Extreme Disturbance Events: Fire in Los Padres National Forest." *Ecological Applications* 7, no. 4 (November 1997): 1252-62.

Murphy, Kyle. "Carmel River, Monterey County." *Wild and Heritage Trout Newsletter* (California Department of Fish and Game), Fall 1995.

National Weather Service. "Lightning." December 22, 1999. Available at http://www.nws.noaa.gov.

Norris, Frank. *The Octopus*. New York: Doubleday, Page, 1901.

Pincetl, Stephanie S. *Transforming California: A Political History of Land Use and Development*. Baltimore: The John Hopkins University Press, 1999.

Reinstedt, Randall A. *More Than Memories*. Monterey CA: Monterey Peninsula Chamber of Commerce Foundation, 1985.

Rinehart, Mary Roberts. *The Circular Staircase*. New York: Farrar & Rinehart, 1921.

Serra, Junípero. *Writings of Junípero Serra*. Vol. 3. Edited by Antonine Tibesar. Washington DC: Academy of American Franciscan History, 1956.

Simon, Ted. *The River Stops Here*. New York: Random House, 1994.

Stevenson, Robert Louis. *Across the Plains with Other Memories and Essays*. New York: Charles Scribner's Sons, 1901.

The Hand Book to Monterey and Vicinity, 1875. Monterey CA: Walton and Curtis, 1875.

U.S. Forest Service. "Lessons Learned from the Marble-Cone Fire." News release, September 24, 1999.

————."Policy Implications of Large Fire Management: A Strategic Assessment of Factors Influencing Costs." U.S. Forest Service, n.d. http://www.fs.fed.us/fire/management.

Vizcaino, Sebastian. *The Voyage of Sebastian Vizcaino to the Coast of California, Together with a Map and Sebastian Vizcaino's Letter Written at Monterey, December 28, 1602*. San Francisco: The Book Club of California, 1933.

Walton, John. *Storied Land: Community and Memory in Monterey*. Berkeley: University of California Press, 2001.

————. *Western Times and Water Wars*. Berkeley: University of California Press, 1992.

"Waterways." *Carmel River Watershed News* 1, no. 1 (October 2001).

Winter Water Quality of the Carmel and Salinas Lagoons, Monterey, CA. Monterey CA: The Watershed Institute, California State University, Monterey Bay, March 29, 2001.

Wood, Samuel E., and Alfred E. Heller. *California Going, Going . . . .* Sacramento: California Tomorrow, 1962.

Also by Ray A. March

NONFICTION

*Alabama Bound: Forty-Five Years
Inside a Prison System*
(University of Alabama Press, 1978)

A Paradise Called Pebble Beach
(Golf Digest, 1992)

California Golf
(Foghorn Press, 1992–93, 1993–94)

Two Bites of the Cherry
(Carmel Publishing Company, 2000)

ANTHOLOGY

The New Book of California Tomorrow
(William Kaufmann, Inc., 1984)